Current Principles and Practices in Association Self-Regulation

Lawrence J. Lad, DBA

with a foreword by Howard H. Bell, CAE
American Advertising Federation
and an introduction by Jerald A. Jacobs
Jenner & Block

This study was made possible by grants from
the ASAE Government Relations Education Fund (GREF)
and The Foundation of the American Society of Association Executives

Published by the
American Society of Association Executives
Washington, DC

Design, editing, composition, proofreading:
    Monotype Composition Company, Inc.
    Baltimore, MD

Library of Congress Cataloging-in-Publication Data

Lad, Lawrence J.
    Current principles and practices in association self-regulation/
Lawrence J. Lad.
        p.   cm.
    Includes bibliographical references (p. 120).
    ISBN 0–88034–050–9
    1. Associations, institutions, etc.—Management—Standards—
United States. 2. Trade and professional organizations—Management—Standards—United States. 3. Associations, institutions, etc.—
United States—Directories. 4. Associations, institutions, etc.—
Law and legislation—United States. I. Title.
AS6. L23 1992
061' .3—dc20
                                        91-34637
                                              CIP

Copyright © 1992 by the American Society of Association Executives.

All rights reserved. No part of this book may be reproduced or transmitted in any form or by any means, electronic or mechanical, including photocopying, recording, or by an information storage and retrieval system, without permission in writing from the publisher.

American Society of Association Executives
1575 Eye Street, N.W.
Washington, DC 20005-1168

Printed in the United States of America.

Contents

Foreword	v
Acknowledgments	vii
Introduction: Legal Issues and Processes in Association Self-Regulation	1
1 Creating a Context: Self-Regulation and Public Policy	18
2 An Historical Perspective of Industry Self-Regulation	22
3 Answering the Basic Questions	44
4 Guidelines for Developing a Self-Regulation Program	65
5 The Direct Selling Association Code of Conduct: A Case Study	74
6 Defining the Self-Regulation Environment	93
Appendix: Descriptions of Selected Self-Regulation Programs	98
Bibliography	121

Foreword

This compendium on self-regulation is truly a milestone in the history of the American Society of Association Executives (ASAE). It is the first time that a comprehensive survey of self-regulation in the association field has ever been undertaken. It was a monumental task for which I applaud the ASAE staff, the Ad Hoc Committee on Self-Regulation, and Dr. Larry Lad of Butler University who developed the research project that made this compendium a reality.

Until now not much has been known about the extent of self-regulation among trade associations. Some were doing it, some were interested, and some were shying away from it for various reasons or knew little about it and what it might do to serve their needs and interests.

In 1984 a most successful ASAE/White House Conference on Self-Regulation focused industry attention on this subject. As a result, the ASAE Board created the Ad Hoc Committee on Self-Regulation to explore programs and make recommendations to the ASAE Board on ways to further advance association-sponsored self-regulation in the public interest.

In 1986 the Ad Hoc Committee spearheaded a second conference on self-regulation, which was also well received. Following this conference, the Ad Hoc Committee recommended to the ASAE Board that it undertake a major study, which the Board approved. The ASAE Foundation agreed to help with initial funding.

As indicated in the report, 898 associations participated in the study, with 252 associations reporting on their involvement in this area. The report covers three basic types of programs: (1) quality and safety standards for products and services, (2) professional licensing and accreditation, and (3) codes of conduct. Each of these areas represents a major activity that we classify as self-regulation, but there is often a lack of agreement on terminology. Ironically, the term *self-regulation* itself is a misnomer. In most cases we are neither talking about *self* nor *regulation* in the traditional sense. What we are really talking about is what associations do for themselves on behalf of their members in the fields of standards, certification, accreditation, or codes of conduct that might otherwise be done by government legislation or regulation.

As this report suggests, regarding governmental action in this area, there are many advantages for associations in adopting the attitude best described by the famed advertising slogan, "Please, mother, we'd rather do it ourselves!"

For most of my professional career, I have been involved with self-regulation programs, and I can personally attest to the fact that such programs do help avoid unnecessary government intervention and regulation; they are far more efficient and effective, far more reasonable and fair, and far less costly than government regulation. Most importantly, such programs provide a real service to government, the public, and the membership of the particular association. They build stature and respect for an industry, an objective sought by every association on behalf of those it represents.

This is why I am so pleased with the completion and the publication of this report. I believe it will help many of my colleagues in the association field, especially those who are not now involved in this area, to consider the opportunities and the benefits that may await them in this general field we call self-regulation. This study will serve as a benchmark for future studies by ASAE that reflect an ever-growing trend by associations to "do it themselves."

One of the important revelations documented in the ASAE-sponsored Hudson Institute study, *The Value of Associations to American Society*, is the key role associations play in serving the public through programs of self-regulation. It is one of the major reasons why the basic conclusion of the Hudson study is that Associations Advance America. It is the reason why I salute everyone who participated in making this report on self-regulation possible.

> Howard H. Bell, CAE
> President, American Advertising Federation
> Chair, ASAE Ad Hoc Committee on
> Self-Regulation
> Washington, DC

Acknowledgments

Life moves on, people evolve, and circumstances change. The idea for this book is at least six years old and almost three years have passed since the data collection process began. The initial concept was to describe the "state of the art" in self-regulatory practices by trade associations and professional societies. Not only was this basic objective fulfilled, but also we were able to put the idea of self-regulation into a context that reflects the crucial role associations play in society—that of serving the "public interest" as collaborators between business, government, and the professions.

This study would not have been possible without the collaborative efforts of many individuals working behind the scenes. In particular, the following members of the ASAE Ad Hoc Committee on Self-Regulation should be recognized for their ideas and encouragement: Chair Howard H. Bell, CAE, American Advertising Federation, Jerald A. Jacobs, Jenner and Block, and Neil H. Offen, CAE, Direct Selling Association, all of Washington, DC. ASAE staff Ann Kenworthy and Publisher Elissa Myers, CAE, and former staff Harris Jordan, Liz Malloy, and Lois Snyderman, who kept me informed and on schedule, are recognized for their support, information updates, and ongoing contact.

At Indiana University, nothing would have moved forward without the able support of my research assistants Sandy Brents, Pam Grohe, and Marianne Lewis. Through them I learned some things I didn't know about management and computers. Thanks also are due to typists Mary Rooks, Michele Shambaugh, and Bev Arthur.

I also want to express appreciation to Dean Jack Engledon and my colleagues at Butler University for their support in the final stages of the project.

Finally, to all individuals who took time to complete the survey and respond to follow-up phone calls, my thanks.

Lawrence J. Lad
Indianapolis, Indiana

Introduction

Legal Issues and Processes in Association Self-Regulation

Jerald A. Jacobs

Nearly 200 years ago, the forefathers believed that government is best when it governs least.[1] James Madison, history's ultimate newspaper columnist, argued eloquently and successfully that good and virtuous people require little governance and are even oppressed by the government that is necessary to control those who would injure others.[2] Current newspaper columnist George Will applies the *Federalist Papers* to today's "big government." He writes: "The problem is not bigness, it is unreasonable intrusiveness, which is a function of policy, not size. Besides, inveighing against big government ignores the fact that government is about as small as it will ever be and ignores the fact that government, though big, is often weak."[3] He argues for reasonable balance of competing values, which often requires limits on liberty and resistance to libertarianism that seeks to maximize freedom for private appetites. This balance is necessary to avoid dissolution of public authority, social and religious traditions, and other restraints necessary to prevent license from replacing durable, disciplined liberty.

This has everything to do with self-regulation, as well as government regulation, since self-regulation—if it is to continue and increase in effectiveness—is essentially quasi-governmental.

This introduction examines some appropriate roles for private and government regulation. Society requires regulation, but regulation can be effected both through public agencies (federal, state, and local governments) in mandatory mechanisms and through private agencies (trade, professional, and other nonprofit associations) in voluntary mechanisms.

Mr. Jacobs is a partner in the law firm of Jenner & Block, Washington, DC, where he heads the firm's association practice group.

The most successful voluntary self-regulation mechanisms have so far included codes of ethics, professional credentialing, and product standards and certification. In many ways, these voluntary mechanisms are superior alternatives to enforced government regulation. These voluntary vehicles for self-regulation share certain general advantages and can best balance competing values, because they are

- conventional mechanisms already accepted, understood, and operating effectively;

- essentially legal and have been endorsed by legislatures, courts, and perhaps most important of all, federal antitrust agencies;

- limited, efficient, and benign because they are operated primarily by expert volunteers;

- involve less delay, red tape, costs, inflexibility, and resistance to innovation than detailed government regulations; and

- often can take advantage of greater expertise and more comprehensive coverage than is possible with governmental resources.

Self-regulation, however, is not without its drawbacks. The most serious and prevalent danger is the antitrust potential of voluntary mechanisms by which rules and interpretations can be applied to block current and potential competitors. In addition, voluntary mechanisms may sometimes lack the incentive to take account of external societal costs. Thus, the balance struck by self-regulatory bodies between internal industry costs and benefits will often not be the same as the optimum economic and social balance that would be achieved if all relevant costs stemming from a proposed action were internalized.

The real and perceived advantages and shortcomings of government and private sector regulation account in large part for the cyclical nature of American governmental reform. Demands for, and implementation of, increased governmental regulation during the Populist, Progressive, New Deal, and Great Society eras were interspersed with periods of heightened emphasis upon the importance of unleashing private sector forces from excessive governmental restraints. Popular recognition that the private sector had failed to cope adequately with the monopolistic power of robber barons, inadequate food safety, the Great Depression, racial discrimination, and poverty fueled the fires of government regulation. New laws and federal agencies designed to rectify private sector shortcomings resulted.

Beginning with the Carter Administration's initiatives on deregulation of the airlines, trucking, and other areas, and continuing on a broader scale with the Reagan and Bush Administrations, the pendulum has once again swung away from government regulation. "Deregulation" has become the watchword, opening up unique opportunities for the private sector to develop and implement adequate voluntary methods of dealing with the conditions that gave rise to mandatory regulation.

Deregulatory efforts have focused upon achieving reduced or modified government regulation because government regulation has occasionally been considered excessive, inefficient, or oppressive. Although organized and grass roots sentiment in favor of deregulation is far from unanimous, both major political parties are engaged in close scrutiny of government regulatory agencies for waste, inefficiency, and unnecessary duplication of private sector initiatives. Leading Democrats and Republicans are actively seeking alternatives to traditional government regulatory activities, providing a receptive environment for innovative approaches to the interaction between government and private regulation.

Practical and ethical obligations accompany this special opportunity. If private, voluntary self-regulation efforts fail, demands for the government to impose its own regulations directly, or upon the voluntary bodies, will begin again. Furthermore, increased societal reliance on self-regulation and decreased governmental scrutiny impose upon private associations the ethical responsibilities attendant upon their role as quasi-governmental entities. Therefore, both practical and ethical considerations dictate that private self-regulatory bodies impose only impartial, reasonable criteria and follow fair procedures in making decisions with powerful economic effects.

Responsible action by private self-regulatory agencies is a necessary step toward increased use of voluntary self-regulation, but it is not sufficient. Supportive actions by the public and government are also required. Specifically, the public must demonstrate a greater awareness of self-regulatory mechanisms that are already in place and must support implementation of their further possibilities.

The required governmental role involves the major deterrent to increased self-regulatory activities: the threat of antitrust lawsuits.

Although a blanket exemption of Department of Justice or Federal Trade Commission scrutiny of association self-regulation is one possible approach, that approach is not politically practical and may not even be substantively appropriate. Instead, what is needed from the administration, Congress and the judiciary is further recognition and endorsement of self-regulation, particularly by more precise definitions of self-regulatory conduct that *does not* constitute violations of antitrust laws. Voluntary self-regulatory bodies need guidance as to what criteria and what procedures they can utilize that will likely insulate them from antitrust liability. Many judicial and administrative pronouncements have praised self-regulation programs over the years,[4] a recent decision of the United States Supreme Court does so with some enthusiasm.[5] However, most of these pronouncements occur as counterpoints to judicial and administrative decisions condemning particular self-regulation programs, or features of those programs, as anti-competitive.[6] The result is a "chilling effect" whenever one reviews the accumulated law on association self-regulation.

To correct for the relative absence of positive assistance and guidelines on self-regulation, the association community should not necessarily seek further intrusion of government into the self-regulatory process. One historian does note that no class of Americans has ever objected to any form of government meddling that appeared to benefit that class. Far from government meddling, what self-regulation seems to need most just now is a "night watchman" approach by government. To achieve this, associations will have to reexamine the reasonableness of their self-regulation criteria and the fairness of their procedures; then, they may have to sell self-regulation to the public and to the government. From that, it is hoped, a favorable climate for self-regulation will result.

Codes of Ethics

Focusing now upon specific vehicles for self-regulation, association codes of ethics may be foremost. Trade, professional, and other associations have long felt the responsibility to foster ethical conduct by establishing and maintaining codes of ethics. An American Medical Association code was established in 1848.[7] In 1926, a collection of nearly 300 codes of ethics of manufacturing, service, and professional associations was published."[8]

More recently, codes of ethics have received renewed emphasis from the negative Watergate era perceptions of a "moral crisis in business,"[9] and the positive opportunities for voluntary self-regulation opened up by the current government deregulation movement.

A 1979 survey showed that 41 percent of associations polled had ethical codes.[10] As a 1980 follow-up survey sponsored by the Ethics Resource Center demonstrated, most association codes have been in existence far longer than have corporate codes.[11] Given this greater experience with and broader scope of association codes, this introduction is directed primarily to association codes of ethics.

Trade, professional, and other association codes of ethics can protect both business and the consumer from conduct that is commonly recognized to be illegal, immoral, or otherwise unacceptable. Ethical constraints developed and applied by one's peers are likely to achieve a higher degree of adherence and support than prohibitions imposed from outside by government agencies.[12]

Generally, ethical codes have been either separately stated or included in association bylaws or articles of incorporation.[13] Associations have required the express or tacit agreement of all members to abide by the code and have attempted to discipline or exclude members who refuse or fail to adhere to a code's provisions.

These codes can be either affirmative, aspirational guidelines, negative, prohibitive lists of "shall nots," or what is probably the best approach, a combination of general affirmative guidelines and specific "don'ts" that focus on particularly undesirable conduct.[14] The *hybrid* code model, for example, is followed by the American Bar Association, the American Medical Association, and the American Institute of Certified Public Accountants.[15] The most effective code approach may well include another hybrid feature, combining regulation of specific actions with disclosure requirements.[16] Typical association codes address such subjects as

- honest and fair business dealings with customers, clients, or patients;

- acceptable levels of safety, efficacy, or cleanliness of products, services, or facilities;

- nondeceptive advertising; and

- maintenance of experienced and trained personnel, performance of competent services, and furnishing of quality products.

As in other areas of self-regulation, care should be taken to avoid any antitrust problems that might arise from the establishment, interpretation, and enforcement of association codes of ethics. The Supreme Court has recognized both the proper role of association self-regulation and the limits defined by the antitrust laws. In an early landmark case, Chief Justice Hughes stated for the Court that

> voluntary action to end abuses and to foster fair competitive opportunities in the public interest may be more effective than legal process . . . [but] the freedom of concerted action to improve conditions has an obvious limitation. The end does not justify illegal means. The endeavor to put a stop to illicit practices must not itself become illicit. As the statute draws the line at unreasonable restraints, a cooperative endeavor which transgresses that line cannot justify itself by pointing to evils affecting the industry or to a laudable purpose to remove them.[17]

Thus, the legality of self-regulatory schemes must be assessed as to their actual anticompetitive effects regardless of their possible procompetitive purpose and good intentions.[18] Basically, codes of ethics face two potential antitrust problems.[19] Use of coercive sanctions such as fines or expulsion to compel adherence may effect an illegal boycott, particularly where *membership* in an association confers singular competitive benefits in a business, profession, or other area. Even in the absence of coercion, the code may itself be an illegal agreement or evidence of an illegal agreement.

Three U.S. Supreme Court rulings held that imposition of sanctions for particular conduct violated the antitrust laws. These rulings involved

- a professional engineers association whose code of ethics prohibited competitive bidding by members,[20]

- a sugar industry association whose code prohibited members from granting secret price rebates, [21] and

- a women's apparel manufacturing association whose code prohibited members from dealing with retailers that handled "pirated" fashion styles.[22]

Two other Supreme Court decisions made it clear that professional association codes of ethics are not exempt from legal constraints even when they are adopted or endorsed by a state. In the *Goldfarb* case, the Court held that a local bar association's minimum fee schedule enforced by a state bar association violates the antitrust laws and is not protected by any "learned profession" or "state action" exemption from such laws.[23] Even though the fee schedule was purportedly only advisory, the Court found that it was, in effect, a "fixed, rigid price floor"[24] and therefore constituted illegal price fixing.

Nevertheless, some have taken solace from a footnote in the Court's decision, which stated:

> The fact that a restraint operates upon a profession as distinguished from a business is, of course, relevant in determining whether that particular restraint violates the Sherman Act. It would be unrealistic to view the practice of professions as interchangeable with other business activities, and automatically to apply to the professions antitrust concepts which originated in other areas. . . . We intimate no view on any other situation than the one with which we are confronted today.[25]

A subsequent Supreme Court case, which was decided on constitutional rather than antitrust grounds, ruled that bar association disciplinary rules against advertising by lawyers were illegal, even though they had been promulgated by the Supreme Court of Arizona.[26] The U.S. Supreme Court did conclude, however, that prohibition of false, deceptive, and misleading advertising, and reasonable restrictions on the time, place, and manner of advertising, would be permissible.[27]

Although a considerable degree of uncertainty regarding the legal limits of association codes of ethics remains, certain guidelines and general principles emerge from a study of the case law. Association ethical proscriptions should not attempt to completely prohibit advertising, competitive bidding, or discounting. Apart from narrowly drawn provisions dealing with deception, they should not attempt to restrict or regulate prices or other terms or conditions of sale. Ethical provisions should be clearly defined standards that are known by all members.

Administration of reasonable and nonrestrictive sanctions for violations of association codes of ethics must be fair and impartial.

Due process procedures should include:

- a written notice to the member stating the alleged violation, proposed sanction, and right to comment or right to a hearing;

- a hearing on the charges, if requested, at which the member may present views personally or through a representative, such as a lawyer; and

- the right to appeal an adverse decision to some body in the association that is distinct from the one that made the original adverse decision.

Basically, these guidelines apply as well to the other self-regulatory vehicles addressed in this introduction: credentialing and standards. However, there are two additional points to be made about ethical codes. First, surveys of associations have demonstrated that one of the chief factors inhibiting the adoption of codes of ethics is the fear of antitrust problems.[28] This indicates once again the need for government to more clearly articulate antitrust constraints and, more important, areas that are *without* constraint. Second, the positive, limited experience of federally authorized private association regulation of the ethical conduct of over-the-counter stockbrokers[29] suggests that this model may be adaptable to other areas.

Credentialing

A fundamental purpose of virtually every professional association—and many trade associations—is to improve the quality of professional competence within the area represented by the association. Credentialing is one major supplement to the codes of ethics just discussed, as well as to educational meetings, publications, and research.

Voluntary credentialing encompasses both certification of individuals who have been tested for proficiency and accreditation of educational institutions that have been approved for specific courses of study. A third kind of credentialing activity—occupational licensing—which is performed by state governments, is generally a mandatory legal condition for employment and, hence, is outside the topic of this introduction on self-regulation.

Association professional certification and accreditation is widespread. A 1965 study reported that 120 private associations engaged in credentialing.[30] Today, the number is probably several times higher. Through credentialing programs, those most familiar with the appropriate educational and ethical qualifications necessary for individuals and institutions can establish and administer curriculum and faculty requirements for accredited institutions and conduct examinations for individuals.

Professional credentialing enhances the prestige, and possibly the earning potential, of certified individuals and accredited institutions. Certification also enables consumers, the government, and other third-party payers for professional services to distinguish between those who have attained specified levels of competency and those who have not. Therefore, association credentialing protects the public by providing a comprehensible and identifiable measure of competency, while aiding the profession by encouraging and recognizing high professional achievement.[31]

The very success of professional credentialing programs in influencing marketplace decisions has invited scrutiny by the Federal Trade Commission and the Department of Justice of alleged illegal practices and has invited private suits by those whose credentials have been denied or revoked. A review of the court decisions in this area reveals that where membership or credentialing confers significant economic benefits to the point of denying those excluded the ability to practice their profession, a court will likely not grant that association the discretion to set arbitrary or unreasonable membership or credentialing criteria.[32]

With regard specifically to self-regulation of the health professions, where professional certification is most widespread, courts appear reluctant to interfere in credentialing criteria except where evidence indicates that commercial interests are involved in addition to professional competence and patient care concerns. This judicial deference manifests itself in the courts' consideration of the reasonableness of challenged health care programs, rather than in the application of any rule that particular provisions are per se illegal under the antitrust laws without regard for reasonableness.[33]

The required qualification criteria at the heart of every credentialing program must be reasonable. The following guidelines should be considered:

- Criteria should be no more stringent than necessary to assure minimum qualifications, especially where credentialing is of significant economic value.

- Criteria must not have the purpose or effect of unreasonably restricting or boycotting competitors.

- Criteria should be established only after reasonable notice and opportunity to participate is afforded to all those who may be affected by credentialing requirements, including potential candidates and users of their services.

In addition to reasonable criteria, credentialing programs must follow reasonable, objective, and impartial procedures, including adherence to the following guidelines:

- Participation should ordinarily be voluntary and open to those who are not members of the association.

- All candidates should be treated equally; it may not be considered fair to exempt current association members from new credentialing requirements.

- While general promotion of a credentialing program is not a problem, associations should not promote credentialed individuals by name or disparage the noncredentialed.

- Credentialing should not be used to "blackball" or limit the number of competitors arbitrarily.

- Denial of credentials should be made by written notice, giving the reasons for denial; opportunity for an appeal in writing or at a hearing should be offered, to be decided by a body other than the one which made the initial decision.

- Decisions on applications should be made by an objective body not composed exclusively of credentialed individuals who might stand to gain financially from a decision affecting competitors.

The emerging law in this area points clearly to this rule: As association professional credentialing programs become more accepted and useful for basing decisions on employment, advancement, assignment of tasks, and reimbursement, then those associations responsible for the programs will be held to increasingly detailed governmental scrutiny of the substantive reasonableness and procedural fairness of the programs. Properly conducted association professional credentialing programs based upon the principle that credentialing exists primarily to benefit and protect the public offer perhaps the best method of self-regulation of professional services as an alternative to government regulation.

Product Standards

The last conventional mode of association self-regulation, and the one that is the most long-standing and successful, is the development of product standards. Standardization involves the development of models or criteria with which the attributes of products or services can be compared.

Nongovernmental standards affect virtually every aspect of modern society, from the width of railroad tracks to the definition of gasoline. One recent commentator noted that

> estimates of the total number of nongovernmental standards currently in use range from 20,000 to 60,000 plus. Standards setting in the private sector is a huge operation involving hundreds of organizations, tens of thousands of individuals, and countless million man-hours of volunteer labor.[34]

Various types of standards include definitions, recommended practices, methods of testing, classifications, and design and performance specifications.[35] Standards are extremely beneficial both to producers, who are able to achieve greater efficiency and interchangeability, and to consumers, who obtain a means to measure the relative value of products and services they buy.

Government procurement and regulatory bodies generally have recognized that they cannot hope to match the specialized expertise and flexibility of private standards-making bodies. State and local governments typically react to this recognition by adopting private standards in a variety of health, safety, building, and other codes. The reaction of the federal government, which has been more mixed, can best be viewed in the context of the November 1, 1982, issuance by the Office of Management and Budget of the revised, final form of OMB circular No. A-119, entitled "Federal Participation in the Development and Use of Voluntary Standards."[36]

This OMB circular provides policy and administrative guidance to federal agencies on (1) using voluntary standards for procurement and regulatory purposes, (2) participating with private organizations to develop such standards, and (3) coordinating executive branch participation in developing voluntary standards.

Briefly, this circular establishes a powerful, though nonbinding, policy preference in which the executive branch, including independent regulatory agencies, relies upon voluntary standards in procurement and regulatory activities, whenever feasible and consistent with law and applicable regulations. The definition of *voluntary standards* includes both "industry" and "consensus" standards, but excludes professional standards of personal conduct, institutional codes of ethics, private standards of individual firms, and standards mandated by law. These voluntary standards are to be given preference over nonmandatory government standards unless there would be significant disadvantages such as adverse effects on performance, cost, or competition.

The OMB circular No. A-119 represents a departure from previous federal efforts to impose government regulation on the development and utilization of private voluntary standards activities. In 1976 and 1977, legislation was introduced in the Senate to regulate voluntary standards development. On December 7, 1978, the Federal Trade Commission proposed an intrusive trade regulation rule that would have established arbitrary substantive and procedural requirements and imposed fines for violations by voluntary standards groups. Congress responded by enacting the Federal Trade Commission Improvement Act of 1980, which removed the Commission's authority to issue trade regulation rules regarding alleged unfair or deceptive acts with respect to voluntary standards and certification activities. The Commission, however, maintained that it still had authority to issue such rules regarding unfair methods of competition and therefore continued to review the voluminous record, with particular emphasis on whether the prior version of OMB circular No. A-119 had resolved any of its efforts to establish general rules for standards-makers in 1985.[37]

Of the three principal areas of association self-regulation discussed here—codes of ethics, credentialing, and product standards—the latter has received by far the most attention from the judiciary, especially in the 1980s. If there is any area of association self-regulation in which a relatively detailed legal history does provide guidance on how to avoid antitrust problems, it is in the area of standards.

Earlier cases involving standards, especially the Supreme Court's 1961 *Radiant Burners* case, established very clearly that the use of standards in a broader price fixing or boycott conspiracy would be found in violation of the antitrust laws with little difficulty.[38]

In 1982, in the now-famous *Hydrolevel* case, the Supreme Court held an engineering society responsible for a several-million-dollar treble damage Sherman Act antitrust claim resulting from the anticompetitive interpretation of the society's standard for boiler fuel cut-off valves when the interpretation put a manufacturer of an innovative valve out of business.[39] The interpretation was issued by a subcommittee volunteer and staff member of the society; the association did not know of the interpretation, did not approve of it, and did not benefit from it. In the context of an association standards case, the Court established the antitrust principle of the responsibility of an organization for antitrust violations of its volunteers or staff acting with no more than the "apparent authority" of the organization.

Other cases involving association standards in recent years have helped define some of the antitrust boundaries of this self-regulation activity and thereby identified "danger zones." In the Supreme Court's 1988 *Allied Tube* case, the Court clarified that the activities of a private standards-making organization are not necessarily immunized from antitrust challenge under the First Amendment antitrust exemption for "petitioning government" even though the organization's standards are widely used by governments; in this case, a vote-packing scheme by commercial interests affected by the organization's standards resulted in an illegal restraint.[40] The *Allied Tube* case and others involving standards have also spoken to the legal need for a sound technical basis for voluntary standards[41] and the need for fair procedures in developing standards.[42]

With this fairly substantial body of law available on antitrust ramifications of association standards programs, one can identify several legal guideposts for these programs:

- Standards must not be used as devices for fixing prices or otherwise reducing competition.

- Standards must not have the effect of boycotting or excluding competitors.

- Standards must not have the effect of withholding or controlling production.

- Design, specification, or construction standards are legally preferred over performance standards.

- Initial formulation of a proposed standard should involve as many interested parties as feasible. This includes manufacturers, distributors, consumers, users, and so forth.

- Once the proposed standard has been formulated, it should be given the widest possible circulation among persons affected by the provisions.

- Care should be taken that all comments on a proposed standard are considered and proper weight be given to them.

- It is incumbent upon any association sponsoring, adopting, administering, interpreting, or enforcing standards to ensure that its standards reflect existing technology and are kept current and adequately upgraded to allow for technical innovation.

- Fees charged in connection with participation in a standardization program must be reasonable as related to the direct and indirect costs involved.

- Membership in groups or organizations sponsoring, promulgating, or administering standardization programs must be open to all competitors.

- Due process should be accorded all parties interested in, or affected by, a standardization program, including suppliers, manufacturers, distributors, customers, and users; due process includes, but is not limited to, the conduct of timely hearings with prompt decisions on claims respecting standards.

- A standards program should not be affected by proprietary brands or marks.

- Standards programs, unless otherwise clearly required—for example, by considerations or safety—should not be used to reduce, restrict, or limit in any manner, the kinds, quantities, sizes, styles, or qualities of products.

- Representations made by standards organizations with respect to testing procedures must be truthful.

- In cases involving challenges to standards, the burden of proof respecting reasonableness is upon those who develop and enforce the standards.

- All standards promulgated by associations must be voluntary, although government entities sometimes adopt standards and make them mandatory.

- Standards should not involve business practices or contract terms—for example, for freight, credit—between sellers and buyers.

Outlook for Self-Regulation

It seems evident that the current political climate is uniquely favorable to encouragement and advancement of association self-regulatory programs. To be successful, the programs must be enlightened, with responsibility to society and regard for legal hazards.

Association self-regulation programs cannot just foster *rules*. They should promote quality, competence, morality, and virtue. When and if they do, they will grow and prosper.

ENDNOTES

1. Thoreau, H.D. *Civil Disobedience*.
2. Madison, James. *Federalist Papers*. pp. 10 and 51.
3. Will, George. *The Pursuit of Happiness and Other Virtues*. p. 45.
4. *See, e.g. Sugar Institute v. United States*. 297 U.S. 553, 598-99 (1936).
5. *Keller v. State Bar of California*. 110 S. Ct. 2228 (1990).
6. *See*, Remarks of Hon. Douglas H. Ginsburg, Office of Management and Budget, in proceedings of *White House Conference on Association Self-Regulation*, p. 14, ASAE.
7. Krum and Greenhill. *The Extent of Industry Self-Regulation Through Trade Association Codes of Ethics*. Antitrust Bull. 379, 380 (March, 1972).
8. E. Heermance. *The Ethics of Business* (1926). Cited in Krum and Greenhill, id. at 379 n. 2.
9. Harris. *Structuring a Workable Business Code of Ethics*. 30 U. Fla. L. Rev. 310 (1978).

10. Opinion Research Corp. *Codes of Ethics in Corporations and Trade Associations and the Teaching of Ethics in Business Schools* (1979).

11. Opinion Research Corp. *Implementation and Enforcement of Codes of Ethics in Corporations and Associations* (1980).

12. Bowen, H. *Social Responsibilities of the Businessman* 98 (1953), Quotes in Krum and Greenhill, *supra* note 7, pp. 379-380.

13. Brebbia, J. Codes of Ethics and Lobbying. Antitrust Comm. of the Bar Assoc. of the District of Columbia Symposium on Trade Associations, *Government Regulation or Self-Regulation: The Outlook for the 70's.*

14. Harris, *supra* note 9, pp. 314-321.

15. *Id.*

16. *Id.* pp. 321-26.

17. *Sugar Institute v. United States.* 297 U.S. 553, 598-599 (1936).

18. *See Sugar Institute, id. Fashion Originators' Guild of America v. FTC,* 312 U.S. 457 (1941); *see also American Medical Association v. United States,* 317 U.S. 519 (1943); *Northern California Pharmaceutical Association v. United States,* 306 F.2d 379 (9th Cir. 1962), *cert. denied,* 371 U.S. 862 (1962); *United States v. Gasoline Retailers Association, Inc.,* 285 F.2d 688 (7th Cir. 1961); *United States v. Utah Pharmaceutical Association,* 201 F.Supp. 29 (D. Utah 1962), *aff'd per curiam,* 371 U.S. 24 (1962).

19. See Lamb, G. and Shields, C. *Trade Association Law and Practice.* Sec 10.9, p. 160 (1971).

20. *National Society of Professional Engineers v. United States.* 453 U.S. 679 (1978).

21. *Sugar Institute v. United States.* 297 U.S. 553 (1936).

22. *Fashion Originators' Guild of America v. FTC.* 312 U.S. 457 (1936).

23. *Goldfarb v. Virginia State Bar.* 421 U.S. 350 (1977).

24. *Id.* p. 781.

25. *Id.* p. 787, n. 17.

26. *Bates v. State Bar of Arizona.* 433 U.S. 350 (1977).

27. *Id.*

28. Krum and Greenhill, *supra* n. 7.

29. 15 U.S.C. Sec. 780-3. See Lamb, G. and Shields, C., *supra* n. 19, at Sec. 10.11.

30. Bradley, J. *The Role of Trade Associations and Professional Business Societies in America.* pp. 95-96 (1965).

31. *See* the extensive discussion of the subject in Wallace, *Occupational Licensing and Certification; Remedies for Denial,* 14 W.M.L.R. 46 (1972).

32. Compare *Salter v. New York Psychological Association,* 248 N.Y.2d. 867 (Ct. App. 1964) (upholding denial) with *Falcone v. Middlesex County Medical Society,* 170 A.2d 791 (N.J. 1961) (overturning denial).

33. *See Viezaga v. National Board of Respiratory Therapy,* 1977-1981 Trade Cases paragraph 61, 274 (N.D. Ill. 1977); *Feminist Women's Health Center, Inc. v. Hohammed,* 415 F.Supp. 1258 (N.D. Fla. 1976).

34. Hamilton. *The Role of Nongovernmental Standards in the Development of Mandatory Federal Standards Affecting Safety or Health,* 56 Tex. L. Rev. 1329, 1332 (1978).

35. *Id.*

36. 47 *Fed. Reg.* 49496 (November 1, 1982).

37. 46 *Fed. Reg.* 10747 (February 4, 1981).

38. *Radiant Burners, Inc. v. Peoples Gas Light & Coke Co.* 364 U.S. 656 (1961); *Standard Sanitary Mfg. Co. v. United States,* 226 U.S. 20 (1912); *National Macaroni Mfs. Assn. v. FTC.* 345 F.2d 421 (7th Cir. 1965); *Bond Crown & Cork Co. v. FTC,* 176 F.2d 974 (4th Cir. 1949); *C-O-Two Fire Equip. Co. v. United States,* 197 F.2d 489 (9th Cir. 1952).

39. *American Society of Mechanical Engineers, Inc. v. Hydrolevel Corp.* 456 U.S. 556 (1982).

40. *Indian Head, Inc. v. Allied Tube and Conduit Corp.* 486 U.S. 492 (1988).

41. *Id.; Consolidated Metal Products, Inc. v. American Petroleum Institute,* 846 F.2d 284 (5th Cir. 1988). *Eliason Corp. v. National Sanitation Foundation,* 614 F2d 126 (6th Cir. 1980).

42. *Id.; but see Northwest Wholesale Stationers, Inc. v. Pacific Stationery and Printing Co.* 105 S. Ct. 2613, 2619 (1985) ("In any event the absence of procedural safeguards can in no sense determine the antitrust analysis.").

Chapter 1

Creating a Context: Self-Regulation and Public Policy

This book is a discussion and analysis of self-regulation carried out by trade associations and professional societies. It provides a history, survey of current practices, and guidelines for developing and enforcing a program.

The study can be considered in a larger context as well. Self-regulation by trade associations and professional societies is a form of public policy in which association members play a quasi-government role in serving the public interest by regulating themselves. It represents a collaborative and cooperative form of policy-making between businesses and government in which the criteria for success are measured in enforceable rules and voluntary standards without the "red tape" and cost of direct government control. In many instances, government is a partner in this voluntary regulatory process, not an adversary. This report is also a story about individual association executives who have assumed a responsibility, even in the face of membership disapproval, to institute professional standards, product quality, and consumer awareness programs for their industry or profession.

The role of associations in self-regulation is highlighted by a casual review of the news. Consider the following headline events:

- Federal courts uphold the baseball commissioner's right to ban Pete Rose from the game after he is indicted for gambling on professional baseball games (code of ethics violation).

- The National Interfraternity Council, Indianapolis, Indiana, seeks self-imposed standards on campus alcohol use after incidents of vandalism and disorderly conduct during fraternity and sorority parties (code of conduct).

- Following the October, 1987 stock market plunge of 500 points, the stock exchanges, the Securities and Exchange Commission, and the National Association of Securities Dealers, Washington, D.C., cooperatively developed a rule to restrict program trading to avoid a similar market fall (technical, cooperative standard).

- Following the violations in recruiting practices, the National Collegiate Athletic Association, Kansas City, Missouri, sanctioned the University of Oklahoma football program prohibiting participation in bowl games and televised games. Similar penalties have been lifted for the Southern Methodist University football program and the University of Kentucky basketball program. Other schools, North Carolina State and the University of Illinois, are now under investigation (procedure rules).

- Following the scandals of Jim Bakker and Jimmy Swaggart, television evangelists proposed and approved a code of ethics for fund-raising and financial management (code of ethics).

- Following the Exxon Valdez oil spill, oil industry executives collaborated to establish the "Valdez principles," a code for improving environmental safety and avoiding another spill.

- Cooperation among industry executives is established for behaviors in accord with the Sullivan principles for business practices in South Africa and the MacBride principles regarding stock market trading and investment banking.

- Food and cosmetic companies have responded to animal rights issues in innovative ways—dolphin-free tuna catches and no use of animals in product testing, respectively.

In these and numerous other examples, trade associations and professional societies are taking steps to address critical issues. The examples and discussion that follow help to explain the behaviors and concerns of these organizations as well as the hundreds of others involved in self-regulation.

The Renewed Attention on Self-Regulation

Increasing interest is being focused on industry and professional self-regulation for a number of reasons. One fundamental influence is the shift in the substance of government regulation from issues of prices (telephone, utilities) and market entry (licensing) to standards (air and water quality, product design and performance, affirmative action, worker safety, executive behavior). With a greater volume of standards being established, the question is, who should do it? Traditionally, government has hired its own experts to set standards and required industry compliance (for example, the Food and Drug Administration, and the Interstate Commerce Commission). While industry should not be allowed to set standards where concerns for public safety are high (nuclear power plants, ethical pharmaceuticals), areas exist in which an industry has the expertise and the information to do its own standard setting (home appliances). Typically, this takes place through industrywide third parties such as business associations. While it entails some form of government oversight, it represents a shift away from complete reliance on government promulgation of rules and industry compliance that is characteristic of direct regulation.

A second factor influencing self-regulation is the realization by industry association executives that an alternative to reacting to what government requires is to take active steps to address problems or issues before mandatory rules are established. The response such as codes of conduct or voluntary standards is encouraged in some instances by proposed legislation that might further constrain an industry's behavior. This is evident in histories of self-regulation in the advertising, direct sales, and home appliance industries as well as in the proposals for improved corporate governance systems developed in the early 1980s.

The rise in self-regulatory activity also reflects a greater reliance on cooperative versus adversarial relationships between business and government. Corporation and trade association executives are more aware of the impact government decisions have on them and actively contact government officials to discuss issues. They are no longer content with a "wait and see" approach when dealing with government, particularly in areas where business has the expertise to set standards or develop credentials. In cooperation with government, systems for rule making, monitoring, and enforcement are being developed. Increasingly, this is taking place on an international scale.

Policy Issues

These trends suggest a number of policy issues. First, self-regulation is *regulatory* policy and therefore requires attention to the roles of key participants, the representation of interests, and the design and performance of the system of rule making, monitoring, and enforcement. Second, self-regulation is *public policy*, requiring scrutiny of how decisions are made and how they affect the public. Accountability, legitimacy, and openness are important concerns. The self-regulatory arena provides an opportunity to explore the weighing of economic, organizational, political, and legal issues in policy making. As a response to external pressures, self-regulation represents cooperative strategy and the use of third parties. Each case involves a unique network of participants and requires negotiated strategies to produce standards and rules. Finally, self-regulation by an industrywide body clearly constitutes a valid, though largely unexplored, instance of associations as "mediating structures." This study is the beginning of that exploration.

Chapter 2

An Historical Perspective of Industry Self-Regulation

The Fundamental Problem

Every society faces the issue of social control of unwanted behaviors—crime, physical abuse, fraud, and improper business tactics. The problem is one of choice: What *means* or *mechanisms* should be used to address the control of these behaviors? Typically, the solution is found in the enactment of laws, the establishment of a legal system, the use of courts, and the assignment of punishment.

The traditional approach to control of improper business behavior in the United States is direct regulation by government. Laws are passed and agencies and commissions are organized to carry them out. Government is the means or mechanism through which social control is established and exercised.

Yet, in some instances, alternatives to total government involvement are possible. Recognizable in the history of industry in the United States is the government-sanctioned presence of industry groups who shape standards, impose rules, and certify and license professionals by themselves. This self-regulation represents an alternative *means* to address such ends as safer products, better qualified professionals, and more adequate consumer information.

Self-Regulation Defined

Industry self-regulation is a regulatory process in which an industry-level organization (a trade association or professional society), as opposed to a governmental or firm-level organization, sets and enforces rules and standards relating to the conduct of firms as well as individuals in the industry (Gupta and Lad 1983). Included in this general definition are standards for products and services (safety, energy use, material quality, advertising copy), professional licensing and accreditation (lawyers, doctors, business schools), and administrative and executive behavior (codes of conduct, financial disclosure).

It is important to recognize that with self-regulation, the primary responsibility for formulation and enforcement of regulatory standards rests with an industry self-regulatory body (association) rather than a government agency. This contrasts sharply with the traditional view of regulation offered by Mitnick (1980, p. 5): "regulation is a process consisting of the intentional restriction of a subject's choice of activity, by an entity not directly party to or involved in that activity. "

With self-regulation, a close relationship usually exists or is developed between the regulatory agency and the industry self-regulating body. The regulator performs an oversight role, may share monitoring and enforcement responsibilities, and can threaten to impose more severe direct regulation should self-regulation prove ineffective. Codes are usually voluntary, and although they do not constitute explicit legal requirements, many are treated as such by the industry.

A self-regulation system is characterized by standard setting (or rule making), monitoring, and enforcement functions. Rarely does industry fully execute all three functions. Typically, committees within industry associations or professional societies propose standards and request government approval through advisory opinions. Monitoring and enforcement procedures are designed to encourage problem resolution within the self-regulatory system before referring the case to government. Often, government serves as the enforcer of last resort. Garvin (1983) illustrates that a "mixed system" entailing shared responsibility between business and government is most common.

As with direct regulation, self-regulation is discussed in a variety of different sources. Industry-specific examples are presented by Chatov (1975) in financial reporting standards, Hunt (1975) in appliance standards, Caves and Roberts (1975) in computer components, LaBarbera (1983, winter) and Boddeywn (1981) in advertising codes and the National Advertising Review Board (NARB), and Dixon (1978) in fire safety. Legal scholars (Michaelson and Dowling, 1983, January 21; Jacobs, 1982) have grappled with the notion of self-regulation as "self-imposed standards setting," and have highlighted court trends in cases of professional credentialing, codes of conduct, and product standards.

What emerges from the literature are notions of industry

endorsement, internal and external control, peer review, a system with mechanisms and checks, a third-party manager of the system, and oversight by government or society. It is clear as well that certain attributes of self-regulation bear a resemblance to direct regulation. The next section traces their parallel histories.

Historical Perspective

Three key historical time periods are important to a discussion of regulation and self-regulation: 1880–1929, 1930–1959, and 1960–present. Each period is characterized by significant changes in the economy (Industrial Revolution, the New Deal, the Great Society) and changes in the law.

1880–1929. The economy of the United States underwent dramatic change and growth during the late nineteenth century. A wave of inventions in manufacturing spurred the growth of textile, machinery, and automobile industries, and were the foundation of processes such as distribution systems that were essential to the evolution of a mass consumer economy. The telephone made immediate communication possible across cities and across the country. The railroads opened up trade with agricultural centers and connected the coasts.

This growth was not without its costs. Newly urbanized workers and children as young as six worked long hours in unsafe factories. Trusts were formed in the railroad, steel, and oil industries causing considerable hardship until the government intervened. Between 1910 and 1920, shakeouts and bankruptcies were occurring in industries where mergers and buyouts were commonplace (Sloan 1964).

Women earned the right to vote in 1916. They were supported by the Populist political movement that fought against unchecked big business growth, but never backed fully the emerging and increasingly militant labor movement. The government, heretofore staffed by patronage appointees, was only beginning to develop a professional civil service.

Economic growth, technological change, and the growing complexity of everyday life generated a number of government and industry responses. Government initiated the first wave of direct regulation, and industry groups and the professions developed mechanisms for self-policing. Table 1 describes the characteristics and examples of regulation and self-regulation initiated during this period.

According to business historian Thomas McCraw (1979), regulation is motivated by the need to "protect the public interest." As the economy grew more complex during the Industrial Revolution, the federal government recognized the need to encourage growth while addressing some of the failures of the marketplace. This is evident in regulation of railroads through the Interstate Commerce Commission in 1887, in banking, where great economic power was coupled with a propensity toward corruption, and in the development of natural monopolies as surrogates for the market, particularly in telephone and telegraph communications and public utilities.

To bust the trusts in oil and other industries, Congress passed the Sherman Act (Michaelson and Dowling 1983, January 21, p. 6). It provides that "(e)very contract, combination in the form of trust or otherwise, or conspiracy, in restraint of trade or commerce among the several states, or with foreign nations, is declared to be illegal...."

In 1915, in response to the emerging consumer economy, the Federal Trade Commission was formed "to promote free and fair competition in interstate commerce through prevention of price-fixing agreements, boycotts, combinations in restraint of trade and other unfair methods of competition" (U. S. Government Manual 1984).

The economic and political change contributed to the involvement of organizations other than industry and government. Business and political associations were becoming an important part of the landscape. They were a part of the American way of life. As Alexis de Tocqueville (1835) noted in his writings about his travels through the United States:

> Americans of all ages, all conditions, and all dispositions constantly form associations. They have not only commercial and manufacturing companies, in which all take part, but associations of a thousand other kinds, religious, moral serious, futile, general or restricted, enormous or diminutive.

The emergence of key professional societies for doctors, lawyers, and accountants in the late 1800s led to credentialing in these professions. As industrial markets grew, technical standards organizations such as Underwriters Laboratories (UL), Oak Brook, Illinios, and the American Society for Testing and Materials (ASTM), New York, New York, were formed to promote part

Table 1. Characteristics and Representative Examples of Regulation and Self-Regulation: 1880–1929

	Direct Regulation	Self-Regulation
Characteristics and Concerns	Maintain competition Reduce corruption Government intervention limited to cases of extreme abuse or need for attention	Professionalization Expansion of markets and need for coordination
Examples	Antitrust Natural monopolies (telegraph, telephone utilities) Federal Trade Commission	Technical standards: auto parts in the 1920s, fire hydrants Some professional coordination Emergence of key organizations, e.g., American Medical Association, 1847; American Institute of Certified Public Accountants, 1887; American Society for Testing and Materials, 1898

Table 1. Characteristics and Representative Examples of Regulation and Self-Regulation: 1930-1959

	Direct Regulation	Self-Regulation
Characteristics and Concerns	Major expansion of government role in economy during New Deal	Response to request by government for self-regulatory system (securities, financial disclosure)
	Industry specific	Attempt to fix prices and markets
	Commission structures	Professionalization of various industries
	Focus on prices and market entry	Emergence of more active state licensing groups
Examples	Food and drug safety	Accounting principles
	Communications	Securities dealers and licensing
	Securities and banking	Airline safety
	Labor relations	Price setting during New Deal via NRA (later found unconstitutional)
	Airlines and other transportation	Licensing
		Early codes of conduct

Table 1. Characteristics and Representative Examples of Regulation and Self-Regulation: 1960–Present

	Direct Regulation	Self-Regulation
Characteristics and Concerns	Broad industry coverage	Market expansion through part interchangeability
	Some commissions (CPSC and Civil Rights)	Safety concerns and consumerism
	Executive agencies (EPA, OSHA)	Energy use
	Some intervention into how business makes decisions (governance, executive responsibility)	Opportunities for cost savings in shared testing
	Economic deregulation (airlines, telephone)	"Proactive" standards
		Attempts to maintain legitimacy
Examples		Stereo equipment
	Externalities (pollution)	Home appliances
		Environmental audits
	Social issues (affirmative action, worker safety)	Paperwork completion
		Motion picture ratings
	Consumer information (labeling, product liability)	Health professional certification
		Health care cost containment

interchangeability and material quality. Fire hydrant nozzles and auto parts were early examples of product standardization.

The courts supported the principle of private industry standard-setting, but watched it closely. According to Michaelson and Dowling (1983, January 21, p. 8):

> Judicial rhetoric regarding product-standard codes had been largely favorable. In 1925 the Supreme Court endorsed product standardization as "admittedly beneficial to the industry and to consumers."[1] Yet in part because manufacturers can establish uniform prices more easily for a standard product,[2] courts scrutinize carefully product-standard codes when challenged as part of a price-fixing conspiracy.[3] Moreover, product-standard codes which compel the boycotting of nonstandard products, and keep them from consumers, have been held to violate the antitrust laws.[4]

Colorful histories of the textile (Galambos 1966), steel, and lumber industries show industry-specific associations also formed to protect industry from organized labor and wage increases, to insure supplies of raw materials, and to address regional disputes among competitors. Trade associations are the most common form of business association. They are defined by *National Trade and Professional Associations* (*NTPA*) as

> ...a nonprofit, cooperative, voluntarily-joined organization of business competitors designed to assist its members and its industry in dealing with mutual business problems in several of the following areas: accounting practices, business ethics, commercial and industrial research, standardization, statistics, trade promotion, and relations with Government, employees, and the general public (*NTPA* 1979).

They typically organize in response to unexpected growth or decline in the industry or by threats from new external competition or government (Pfeffer and Salancik 1978). As Wilson (1973) notes:

> A review of available, but by no means exhaustive or representative, accounts of early trade associations suggests that it was in those industries characterized by fragmentation, competition, and localism that trade organizations principally emerged. Associations formed disproportionately, it appears,

in those industries that were unable to achieve control over their resources and markets by growth or merger.

His ideas are supported by Whitney's (1934) survey of eight trade associations that concluded "such groups have been formed more often in industries with unsatisfactory rather than satisfactory profit levels."

Between 1860–1900 these groups were characterized as "dinner-club associations" (Galambos 1966). They had no professional staff and did little to improve the profitability of their respective industries. Over time they became more professional and more narrowly defined along industry-specific lines such as home appliances, machine screws, asphalt pavement, and pharmaceuticals. This form of organization eventually became involved in self-regulation.

1930–1959. The Depression is typically presented as an economic crisis—thousands of businesses folded and hundreds of thousands of individuals were out of work. Yet, the ramifications affected the political system in a major way. The central government was looked to and relied upon to be the mechanism to rejuvenate the economy. The New Deal programs of the mid-1930s reflected a Keynesian view that government stimulation of the economy could influence economic growth. These programs and the economic climate of the times

- spawned a major wave of new direct regulation by government,

- sanctioned government-supported work programs,

- contributed to the growth of virtually hundreds of business and trade associations,

- allowed for systematic self-regulation in some areas, and

- served as an impetus to expand corporate involvement in government.

Table 1 lists characteristics and examples of direct regulation and self-regulation during this period. The need for an expanded role of government in the New Deal economy after the Depression gave rise to regulation aimed at eliminating the chaotic and destabilizing competition in the newly emerging air transportation and broadcasting industries, at protecting investors in banks and securities, and at ensuring consumer safety in food and drugs.

During the 1930s, self-regulation emerged on a number of fronts. The Securities and Exchange Commission (SEC) was formed with the explicit charter to regulate the self-regulatory bodies in the industry, including NASD for licensing traders, the Accounting Principles Board (APB), Fairfield, Connecticut, and the American Institute of Certified Public Accountants (AICPA), New York, New York, for financial disclosure, and the stock exchanges. The justification for this was that the industry, not government, had the expertise to develop standards and that government should essentially play a watchdog role (Chatov 1978).

During this period, numerous trade associations developed codes of conduct for their membership. Professional licensing emerged in the real estate industry. An example of price-setting self-regulation emerged with the passage of the National Recovery Act (NRA). The Act, developed to stimulate the economy after the Depression, allowed industry representatives to meet together to set prices and inventory levels. The NRA was later judged unconstitutional. According to Wilcox and Shepherd (1975):

> The NRA approved 557 basic codes, 189 supplementary codes, 109 divisional codes, and 19 codes entered into jointly with the Agricultural Adjustment Administration—a grand total 874. The codes spelled out more than a thousand different kinds of provisions for the regulation of 150 different types of competitive practices. They controlled terms of sale, prices, markets, production, capacity, and the channels of distribution. In the name of fair competition, they required adherence to practices that the Federal Trade Commission and the courts had held to be unfair. Industry by industry, they were designed by a majority to curb the competitive propensities of an obstreperous minority. Item by item, they copied the pattern of the standard European cartel.

Wilcox and Shepherd (1975) noted that while the NRA was a noble attempt to stabilize prices and promote production, it graphically illustrated the effects of suspending antitrust. Since it was unsuccessful, it hindered the development of self-regulation in other areas.

In the courts, self-regulation and business codes were given a careful review. As Michaelson and Dowling (1983, January 21, p. 9) point out:

> The attitude of the courts regarding codes has been ambivalent. As early as 1936, the Supreme Court in *Sugar Institute v. United States*[5] recognized the desirability of association self-regulation as "(v)oluntary action to end abuses and to foster fair competitive opportunities in the public interest (which) may be more effective than legal processes."[6]
>
> Yet the court struck down the Sugar Institute's ban on secret price concessions on sugar sold by refiners, noting that the provision went beyond the removal of abuses and became itself an obstacle to competition.
>
> Likewise, in *Fashion Originators' Guild*,[7] guild members attempted to foster competition through increased incentives to clothing designers by refusing to deal with merchants who traded in "pirated" styles. The Supreme Court ignored the manifestly procompetitive purpose of the guild's code provisions, preferring instead to focus on their anticompetitive effects. These included a reduction in the number of intermediaries with which both manufacturers and retailers could deal, and the suppression of competition in the sale of unregistered designs.[8]
>
> As with other types of codes, good intentions of product-standard codes have not immunized them when the effect is anticompetitive. For example, the National Macaroni Manufacturers Association attempted to respond to a worldwide shortage of durum wheat, the major ingredient in high quality macaroni, by suggesting that its members use a blend of other types of wheat.[9] A federal appellate court held that this arrangement produced the "result of depressing the price of an essential raw material, (and thus) violate(d) the rule against price-fixing agreements."[10]

According to McQuaid (1982) and McConnell (1966), corporate executives were closely involved in program planning in the New Deal economy. Roosevelt knew he needed their expertise and support so he appointed many to key positions and sought the advice of numerous others. For business executives, gaining access through regular contacts with White House officials, professionalizing the agencies and newly formed commissions, and sharing ideas on temporary committees represented a new responsibility. Additionally, their involvement was instrumental in getting the economy moving and became a foundation for business participation in government during World War II.

1960 to Present. The 1960s represent another turning point. Post-World War II economic growth expanded the consumer economy and created rising expectations. The Great Society social programs conceived in a period when steady growth appeared continuous were possible in an expanding economy. Government took on a role of social intervention. Influenced by the emerging public interest groups speaking for environmental, consumer, and equal opportunity causes, it instituted a wave of social regulation.

This "new" regulation affected virtually all industries and was aimed at issues of environmental protection, worker and product safety, pension plan funding, corporate governance, and discrimination. During this period, deregulation occurred over economic activity in the airline, trucking, and telephone communications industries. Table 1 shows examples of direct regulation and self-regulation during this era and describes their major characteristics during this period.

Two reactions to the onslaught of public interest legislation were the growth in the number of corporate offices in Washington, D. C. between 1968 and 1975, and the reemergence of another form of business association, the peak association. While characterized by Wilson (1980) and Ranney (1968) as those business coalitions comprising either top level business executives (the Committee for Economic Development) or national groups of business executives (the Chamber of Commerce, and the National Association of Manufacturers), no commonly accepted definition exists. Lad (1981) defined a peak association as a heterogeneous (nonindustry specific) coalition of top executives voluntarily organized to develop "business" or community positions, and to access top government officials on issues of economic, business, or community interest. Included in this definition are organizations such as the Business Round Table and counterparts in Massachusetts and Minnesota (McQuaid 1981), and organizations of top executives from cities such as Chicago (Chicago United), Pittsburgh (the Allegheny Conference), and Boston (Boston Vault). Not included in this group are such large "umbrella" associations (Weidenbaum 1981) as the National Association of Manufacturers (NAM), Washington, D.C., or the Association of Reserve City Bankers, Washington, D.C., as they represent more homogeneous groupings of manufacturers and bankers. The U.S. Chamber of Commerce, Washington, D.C., a general business trade association comprising local and state chambers of commerce, does not qualify as it is not staffed by top executives and its mission is predominantly educational. It also is heavily represented by retail, restaurant, and small business interests. Peak associations are not limited strictly to business organizations. Trist (1978) has identified a number of community-based coalitions of leaders from labor, business, and government that mobilize resources and address critical issues of community survival. Among these are the Jamestown Area Labor Management Committee, the Greater Philadelphia Partnership, and Sudbury 2001.

Corporate conduct was under considerable scrutiny during this period. Incomplete disclosure of corporate financial performance by auditing professionals influenced the opening of the Metcalf hearings in 1972 and spawned the establishment of the Financial Accounting Standards Board (FASB). Scandals such as the bribing of foreign officials by Lockheed led to the passage of the Foreign Corrupt Practices Act. The attention to business ethics gave rise to the formation of the Ethics Resource Center in Washington, D.C., to serve as a clearinghouse for information on business codes of conduct. For a short time, the business community's malfeasance was put aside while the American public watched the Watergate affair unfold and President Nixon resign.

Concern over consumer protection and safe products saw self-regulation expand in the 1960s and 1970s. Not only did the number of technical standards grow (stereo equipment, home appliances, toys, comic books), but also more professional groups sought certification (health care professionals, ophthalmologists). Moreover, institutional standards were developed, including firm-level codes of conduct, revised procedures for corporate governance, and corporate involvement in public institution performance (school curriculum, health care costs).

While the self-regulatory activities of the consumer era did stimulate competition, provide information for consumers to compare products, and encourage more efficient manufacturing, distribution, and consumer complaint systems, failures of some systems are evident. Discussed by Nader and Maier (1983), these include:

- The *Hydrolevel* case in which a proposed boiler shut-off valve was determined by an association committee, American Society of Mechanical Engineers (ASME), as not meeting standards. The

Supreme Court determined that the committee members acted unfairly and in their self-interest by not approving the valve. These individuals were executives in a competitive firm that would have been affected had the valve been approved.

- The American National Standards Institute (ANSI) and the American Gas Institute (AGI) failed to approve a retrofit automatic vent damper for gas furnaces, resulting in higher energy costs for millions of consumers in the early 1970s.

- The Illuminating Engineering Society develops standards for lighting in public buildings. According to estimates, overlit buildings cost taxpayers more than $3.5 billion yearly.

- Aluminum wiring, approved by industrywide standards bodies, was installed in more than 2 million homes between 1965–1972. It is a significant fire hazard.

Consumerists believe that mistakes and the stifling of innovation are endemic to the private standards area. They argue for more democratic, consumer representation on standards committees.

As a result of these and other failures, legal scrutiny over the range of self-regulation that appeared became intense. As Michaelson and Dowling (1983, January 21) describe:

> It was against this backdrop of relatively benign antitrust experience that a series of troubling events transpired in the 1970s and early 1980s, events which significantly altered federal law and enforcement policy governing both professional and trade associations. Following a wave of Justice Department attacks on professional codes in the early 1970s,[11] the Supreme Court held in 1975—to the surprise of many observers[12]—that self-regulation of the learned professions is subject to the antitrust laws. In *Goldfarb v. Virginia State Bar*,[13] the Court invalidated a bar association's fee schedule, characterizing it as illegal price-fixing. The Court rejected widely accepted arguments that professional services are (1) not trade or commerce subject to the Sherman Act; (2) essentially local in nature and thus not interstate commerce; and (3) the source of professional ideals and values inconsistent with the narrow economic values expressed in the antitrust laws. Yet despite the application of

the Sherman Act to professionals, Chief Justice Berger, writing the Court's opinion, acknowledged in *Goldfarb* that: "It would be unrealistic to view the practice of professions as interchangeable with other business activities, and automatically to apply to the professions antitrust concepts which originated in other areas."[14]

Thus the Court in *Goldfarb* admonished against blind application of existing antitrust principles to professions, and specifically acknowledged that the public service aspect of professional practices might require treatment not normally available under the antitrust laws.[15]

Shortly after *Goldfarb*, in *National Society of Professional Engineers v. United States (NSPE)*[16] the Supreme Court invalidated an ethical canon prohibiting competitive bidding for engineering services.[17] More far-reaching than the specific holding, however, was the Court's pronouncement, in an opinion written by Justice Stevens, that only *competitive* factors could be considered when evaluating the legality of professional canons under the antitrust laws. In other words, the Court indicated that safety and other public interest factors are irrelevant to the validity of ethical and other codes under the antitrust laws.[18] Thus the Court effectively disregarded its own admonition in *Goldfarb* to take into account the public-interest aspects of professional codes.

In 1982, in *Arizona v. Maricopa County Medical Society*,[19] the Court again ignored its *Goldfarb* admonition and held that a medical society maximum fee arrangement, which specified amounts above which a physician could not charge and still be reimbursed by the insurance company, was *per se* illegal. The holding of *per se* illegality precluded the medical society from presenting evidence of the fee arrangement's reasonableness, despite the comparative newness and voluntary nature of the arrangement, and the substantial public-interest justifications for limiting medical fees that were proffered in support of it.[20]

Thus in six short years, professionals have traveled from exemption, through a narrow, policy-free, competitive-effects determination, to a Supreme Court holding that even well-intentioned and economically efficient efforts by associations to further the public interest through innovative, choice-enhancing service alternatives can be *per se* illegal.

A comparably drastic change recently took place regarding

civil liability of trade associations under the Sherman Act in relation to codes. In *American Society of Mechanical Engineers, Inc. v. Hydrolevel Corp.*,[21] the Supreme Court held that trade associations can be subject to treble damage liability for acts of their members, even if the association is unaware of, does not ratify, and does not benefit from, the acts. Such liability, the Court held, may be based on apparent authority standing alone. In other words, so long as a third party believes in good faith that the association member is acting on behalf of the association, the association can be liable even though it never authorized, ratified, or derived any benefit from the member's antitrust violation.[22] *Hydrolevel* appears to portend very substantial prospective liability for trade associations, and may discourage association efforts to protect the public interest through business and professional codes.

Another legal expert, Jacobs (1982) has identified similar trends in the professional credentialing area. He cites the following cases and court rulings as indicators that associations need to pay close attention to how rules, particularly those entailing sanctions, are enforced:

In *Silver v. New York Stock Exchange*, 373 U.S. 341 (1963), the U. S. Supreme Court invalidated the self-regulation activity of the New York Stock Exchange in denying telephone line access to two Texas securities dealers primarily because the NYSE used inadequate "due process" in its self-regulatory activity; in *Gibson v. Berryhill*, 411 U. S. 564 (1973), the U. S. Supreme Court addressed the licensing and ethical restraint activities of the Alabama Board of Optometrists and invalidated those activities in part because adequate procedures had not been used to minimize economic interest and professional bias; in *Falcone v. Middlesex County Medical Society*, 34 N.J. 582, 170 A.2d 791 (1961), a county medical society's decision to exclude a physician's license—and thereby deny hospital privileges—was overturned primarily on substantive grounds, but the court also took issue with the fact that the decision was based upon an "unwritten rule" of the society; likewise in *Pinsker v. Pacific Coast Society of Orthodontists*, 12 C.3d 541, 526 P.2d 253 (1974), the court noted that exclusionary practices were unreasonable and because, "In applying a given rule in a particular case, the society acted in an unfair manner"; in *McCreery Angus Farms v. American Angus Association*, 379 F.Supp. 1008, 1010 (S.D. Ill. 1974), a case involving association rules for pure-bred livestock, the court specifically noted that private regulation must not be based upon "old, ad hoc, informal and pro forma committee procedures bordering upon the arbitrary"; finally, in *Blalock v. Ladies Professional Golf Association*, 359 F.Supp. 126, 1268 (N.D. Ga. 1973), a federal court overturned disciplinary action against a professional golfer (accused of moving up her ball in a tournament) because the application of ethical standards was based upon "a completely unfettered, subjective, and discretionary determination of an exclusionary sanction by a tribunal wholly composed of competitors."

Current Issues in Self-Regulation

From the literature and the historical and legal review of the major regulatory and self-regulatory eras, some critical observations emerge for the development of a model.

- Self-regulation as policy has both a macrolevel and microlevel of analysis.

- Critical legal, economic, organizational, and political conditions influence the possibility for, and process of, self-regulation.

- Self-regulation is observable as a process through reactions to conditions, actions by key participants, and assessment of performance.

The historical and legal review highlighted two levels of analysis for self-regulation. For the *macrolevel*, the focus of attention is on the *appropriateness* of self-regulation as a mechanism for controlling business behavior. Most typically it is at this level that government policymakers operate. This level of analysis questions the public policy impact of the choice, and asks where self-regulation can happen and where it cannot. For example, government would not consider self-regulation appropriate in cases where industries could fix prices or unfairly restrain market entry. Moreover, it would not endorse self-regulation in cases where public safety was threatened, as in the case of nuclear power plants or pharmaceutical testing. Yet, as in the case of securities trading in the mid-1930s, government recognized that the industry knew more about how it operated than government did; consequently, the securities trading industry could be encouraged to develop its own licensing and policing system. This was an appropriate area for self-regulation because it did not threaten public safety, and served the public interest by not adding the burden of professional licensing and stock exchange management to government. Furthermore, it allowed the Securities and Exchange Commission to focus on other issues such as promotion of the industry and prosecution of blatant violations.

Once government accepts the idea that self-regulation in an area is appropriate, action must occur at another level. The *microlevel* of analysis draws attention to procedures and processes that organizations (such as associations) engage in to develop and run the system. It is at this level that nongovernment policymakers operate. They address such issues as the design of a self-regulation system's components, procedural fairness, representation on committees, due process, and other considerations. What is notable here is the interaction between the macrolevel and microlevel of analysis. In principle, it appears that macrolevel approval is required before the microlevel system begins to operate. The choice of whether to allow self-regulation in an area needs approval as a concept or idea before the system is designed or initiated. This foreshadows associations engaging in two sets of actions: those directed toward influencing government to view self-regulation as appropriate, and those aimed at developing a system that is acceptable by its membership and government.

The history and literature suggest that critical contextual conditions are essential to the emergence of self-regulation. Economic pressures give rise to the possibility for self-regulation, and legal limitations in antitrust law and court findings shape the parameters of the system. Recognition of the threat of government intervention or the opportunity for expanded markets through part interchangeability or professional licensing can trigger a response by industry for standards or codes. Yet, the extent of the code to enforce membership behavior is limited by law.

According to the American Society of Association Executives, the following types of self-regulation systems are possible:

> **Accreditation.** A process by which an association or agency evaluates and recognizes a program of study or an institution

as meeting certain predetermined standards or qualifications. It applies only to institutions and their programs of study or their services.

Certification. A process whereby an individual is tested and evaluated in order to determine his mastery of a specific body of knowledge, or some portion of a body of knowledge.

Standardization. A process by which a product is assessed against some standard of performance or quality.

Code of Conduct. A statement of principles describing expectations about behaviors of industry (or firm) participants. Often it delineates illegal or unethical behaviors, and frequently includes a process for enforcing such expectations (sanctions, fines, expulsion).

For codes of conduct, accreditation, credentialing, and product standards, the antitrust concern affects both the rules-setting process and the enforcement abilities of the association. Yet, some distinctions are important. In the credentialing area, the focus of attention in the rules stage is on the question of whether the rules or standards themselves restrain trade. As Jacobs (1982) comments:

> The U. S. Supreme Court has disavowed virtually any special consideration for association self-regulation programs merely because they are conducted in professions rather than in businesses. It has been willing to hold several such programs anticompetitive *per se*, when they involved professional fees, without analysis of potentially overriding social or economic justification. Lower court and agency rulings specifically involving credentialing have exclusively utilized the *reasonableness* test method of analysis and have focused upon the economic effects of challenged credentialing determinations in reviewing them judicially and deciding whether credentialing criteria are reasonable and credentialing procedures are fair.

For product standards, the rules-making issue is the representation of members on the committees that set the rules. Here, the real implication of the *Hydrolevel* case noted earlier becomes apparent. Associations must actively show that their committee structure is representative and unbiased, or they may be liable for antitrust damages. Michaelson and Dowling's (1983, January 21) analysis puts this idea in legal perspective:

> Regarding the *Hydrolevel* problem, associations should recognize that the Supreme Court declined to "delineate...the outer boundaries of the antitrust liability of standard-setting organizations for the actions of their agents committed with apparent authority." It should be noted that *Hydrolevel* involved an unappealing factual setting vis-a-vis the association. The jury found that the ASME had indeed ratified its members' violations. Moreover, the violating members were chairman and vice chairman of the subcommittee responsible for drafting and interpreting ASME business codes. In an appropriate factual context, the Court might be willing to reduce the scope of liability created by that decision.

At the enforcement stage for credentialing, the issue is whether the association has the ability to exclude a member or take a license away. This is illustrated in *Silver v. New York Stock Exchange* and other cases noted in the earlier section. For product standards, the enforcement concern is with the appropriateness of the private standards-setting organizations taking on enforcement responsibilities. Both Jacobs (1982) and Gilbert (1972) contend that while the courts are approaching the issue on a case by case basis, they are generally finding *per se* violations rather than addressing public interest issues that would allow expectations on *reasonableness* criteria.

The association must also be careful to incorporate due process procedures into the system. The minimum requirements to meet elementary due process safeguards suggested by Braemer (1969) include (1) reasonable notice of the charges against the member, (2) fair notice of the hearing upon the member, (3) a fair opportunity to hear the evidence and confront and cross-examine witnesses against the member, (4) a fair opportunity to refute the charges against the member, and (5) a hearing before an unbiased tribunal. Evident from this discussion is the recognition of the existing and potential legal constraints associations face in developing a self-regulation system.

To be sure, once the economic opportunity is recognized and the legal limitations understood, organizational and political processes are the mechanisms by which the process is carried out. Business associations play a critical role. Using organization and political skills, they influence government to accept the concept of self-regulation. They develop the system of rules and procedures for carrying them out, and they influence their membership to approve and participate in the system. Additionally, they operate, maintain, and adjust the system over time.

The final issue to note from the historical review of the development of self-regulation is that it is observable, or analyzable, as a process with distinguishable elements. Self-regulation can be viewed as a response to a set of conditions (context) from which actions (behavior) are initiated. These actions produce outcomes or results (performance) that influence new conditions and actions.

ENDNOTES

    1. *Maple Flooring Manufacturers' Association v. United States.* 268 U.S. 563 (1925).
    2. *See Milk and Ice cream Can Institute v. FTC.* 152 F. 2d 478 (7th Cir. 1946).
    3. *Id.* p. 484.
    4. *See, e.g., Radiant Burners, Inc. v. Peoples Gas, Light & Coke Co.* 364 U.S. 656 (1961) (alleged wrongful refusal to certify safety, utility, and durability of plaintiff's gas burners restrictive of competition).
    5. 297 U.S. 553 (1936).
    6. *Id.* p. 598.
    7. *Fashion Originators' Guild of America, Inc. v. FTC,* 312 U.S. 457 (1941).
    8. *Id.* p. 465.
    9. *National Macaroni Manufacturers Association v. FTC.* 345 F. 2d 421 (7th Cir. 1965)
    10. *Id.* p. 426.
    11. *See, e.g., United States v. American Institute of Certified Public Accountants, Inc.* 1972 Trade Cas. (CCH) 74,007 (July 6, 1972); *United States v. American Institute of Architects,* 1972 Trade Cas. (CCH) 73,981 (June 19, 1972); *United States v. American Society of Civil Engineers,* 1972 Trade Cas. (CCH) 73,950 (June 1, 1972).
    12. *See, e.g., Goldfarb v. Virginia State Bar,* 497 F. 2d 1, 13-15 (4th Cir. 1974); Note, 11.
    13. 421 U.S. 773 (1975).
    14. *Id.* p. 788 n. 17.
    15. *Id.*

16. 435 U.S. 679 (1978).
17. *Id.* p. 684-85.
18. *Id.* p. 688, 691.
19. 102 S. Ct. 2466 (1982).
20. The Maricopa County Medical Society argued that the system benefitted consumers by enabling insurance carriers to calculate and to limit more efficiently the risks they underwrite.
21. 102 S. Ct. p. 2482.
22. *Id.* p. 1948. In *Hydrolevel*, the ASME was held liable for treble damages for the antitrust violations of the chairman and vice chairman of its code-drafting subcommittee. These members, one of whom was a competitor of the plaintiff, sought an interpretation from the subcommittee which suggested falsely that the plaintiff's product was unsafe. Subsequently, the interpretation was distributed to customers in order to discourage them from purchasing the plaintiff's product.

Chapter 3

Answering the Basic Questions

Background on the Study

The self-regulation research project was initially conceived by the ASAE Ad Hoc Committee on Self-Regulation in January 1988 as a means for determining the scope, range, and quality of self-regulation efforts by trade associations and professional societies. Considerable self-policing activity in diverse areas such as product standards, certification, and codes of ethics was taking place, yet no clearinghouse of information on the process and pitfalls of developing a program was available. The basic goals of the study were to compile a comprehensive catalog of existing self-regulation programs and to determine the critical characteristics of the successful self-regulation programs. The key questions driving the study were:

- Why does self-regulation occur?

- What is self-regulation?

- How many programs exist? How are they different?

- What roles do associations play in self-regulation?

- What are the conditions for success?

- What explains the failure of some attempts at self-regulation?

- What are the current critical issues and concerns with self-regulation?

An extensive 45-question survey questionnaire was developed by the author with input from Ad Hoc Committee members and

ASAE Government Affairs staff. ASAE completed two survey mailings to associations across the country and abroad. The first went out in July 1988 (to approximately 3,000 associations) and the second in January 1989 (to 2,000 organizations that did not respond to the first survey). A third mailing to 10 associations with existing programs not in the data base was initiated in March 1990.

The survey generated a 30 percent overall response rate and documented examples of more than 270 programs. Upon review, 252 of the completed questionnaires were sufficient for entry into the data base.

What Is Self-Regulation?

One of the obvious issues confronting ASAE, association professionals, government regulators, lawyers, and researchers in discussions about self-regulation is the *variety of definitions* individuals associate with the practice. Some approach the area in a rather focused fashion and highlight specific forms (codes of conduct, technical standards, certification, or licensing rules). Others see it as a more inclusive term, covering the array of different types of self-policing.

The survey used an open-ended question to generate a list of the various terms and conceptions. Quite predictably, the responses covered the spectrum from very specific to very general. To be sure, an unexpected distinction was the degree of emphasis about the role that government approval or oversight played in the process. Many saw government completely removed from the process; some recognized the collaborative nature of a number of self-regulatory systems even if government simply served in an oversight role.

To address the two schools of thought about self-regulation (no government versus cooperation with government), two separate definitions with similar scales were presented. The respondents were asked to agree or disagree with the definitions. The definition that emphasized no government involvement was given as follows:

> Self regulation is a private alternative to direct regulation by government. It is a process whereby an interorganizational network (such as a trade association, professional society, or other third party) sets and enforces standards relating to the conduct of firms and/or individuals in an industry or profession.

Out of 251 respondents, 206 agreed with this definition, 12 disagreed, and 33 were neutral. In the written comments, some noted that self-regulation would not work in all cases; others highlighted the fact that government efforts in some areas would be too costly; still others emphasized that industry insiders were best suited to self-policing because of their expertise and understanding of the industry or profession.

The definition that emphasized cooperation with government was given as follows:

> Self-regulation is a form of cooperative regulation wherein industry associations and/or professional societies work together with government regulators and other groups to form rules, standards, and enforcement mechanisms relating to the conduct of firms and/or individuals in an industry or profession.

Out of 245 respondents, 98 agreed with this definition, 67 disagreed and 80 were neutral. Comments were at the extremes. One perspective was that if government is involved, it isn't self-regulation but cooperative regulation. Another set of views accurately noted that many self-regulation systems operate independently but with government approval and oversight.

Two of the frequently referred to definitions in academic literature are offered here.

> Industry self-regulation is a "regulatory process in which an industry-level organization (such as a trade association or professional society), as opposed to a governmental or firm-level organization, sets and enforces rules and standards relating to the conduct of firms as well as individuals in the industry" (Gupta and Lad 1983).

Included in this definition are standards for products and services (safety, energy use, material quality, advertising copy), professional licensing and accreditation (lawyers, doctors, business schools), and administrative and executive behavior (codes of conduct, financial disclosure).

> Self-regulation exists when industry members jointly pursue regulatory standard-setting activities in the absence of explicit requirements. A variety of actions, including the disclosure

of product information, the policing of deceptive practices, the establishment of minimum standards of safety and quality, the grading of products, and the creation of industry codes of conduct, falls under this heading (Garvin 1983).

Both definitions correctly note that the primary responsibility for the formulation and enforcement of regulatory standards rests with an industry self-regulatory body (such as an association) rather than a government agency.

Figure 1 suggests a way of looking at self-regulation in its various forms. Depending on the regulatory issue, business and government are involved at varying degrees. Pure self-regulation fits in the extreme right of cell 2; pure direct regulation is at the extreme of cell 3. It is important to note, however, the many instances where business and government share responsibility for the regulatory process. Also critical is the growth of activity in cell 4 where high-risk technologies require *both* parties to share in the process of rule making and enforcement.

Why Self-Regulation?

In discussions and debates about business ethics and regulatory reform, limited consideration is given to encouraging self-regulation or self-policing by industry associations and professional societies. Yet, a closer look at regulatory history uncovers some rich information. Self-regulatory history shows the dramatic parallels with eras of direct regulation—technical and professional standards organizations evolved during the Industrial Revolution, administrative and safety standards groups took root during the New Deal era, and institutional codes, consumer awareness programs, and emerging professional codes have been shaped since 1960. Of survey respondents, only 72 systems were formed prior to 1960; 95 were founded between 1961–1979; and 60 developed since 1980.

Three traditional rationale are offered for self-regulation. The first is that self-regulation is essentially *market driven*. Technical standards organizations arise to support industry leaders, allowing for part interchangeability, compatibility, and cost savings. Professional codes or credentialing insures minimum competency and promotes ongoing education and development.

The second rationale is that self-regulation can create an *identity* for an industry or legitimize a profession. In some cases, it may

Figure 1. Government and Industry Involvement in the Regulatory System

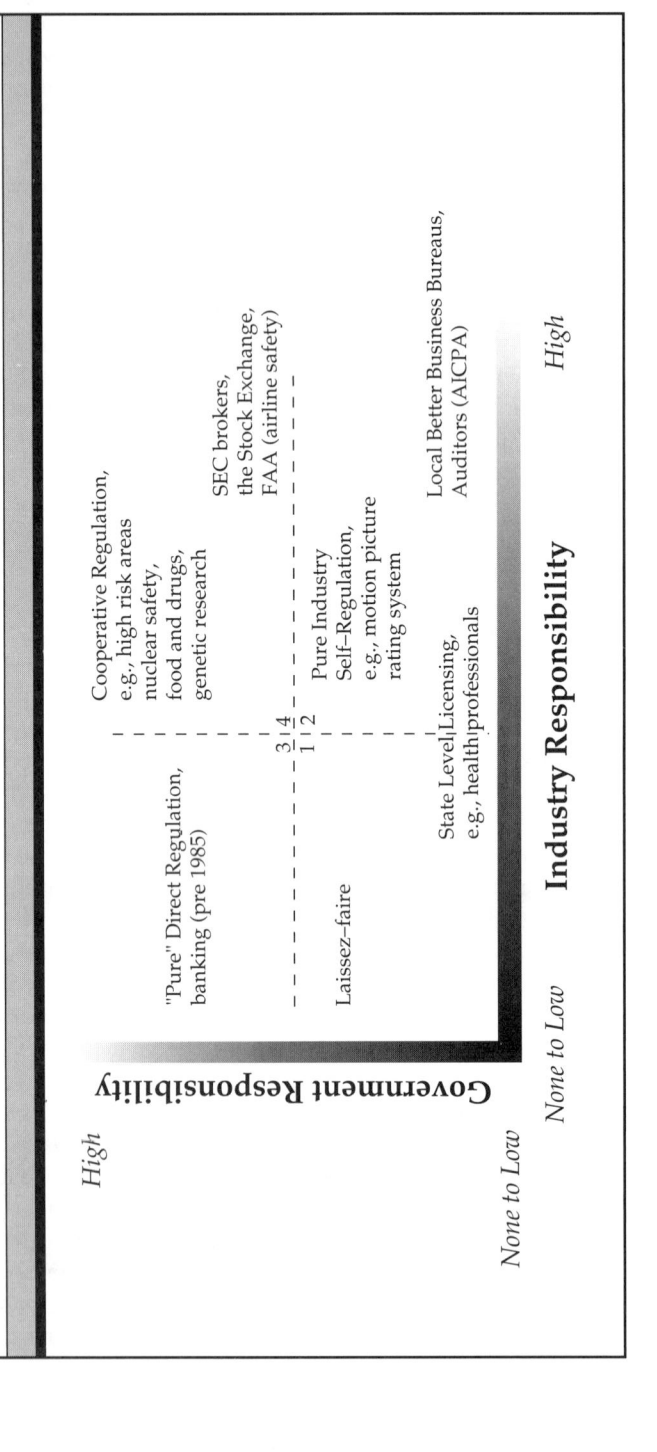

Cooperative Regulation, e.g., high risk areas nuclear safety, food and drugs, genetic research

SEC brokers, the Stock Exchange, FAA (airline safety)

"Pure" Direct Regulation, banking (pre 1985)

Pure Industry Self-Regulation, e.g., motion picture rating system

3 | 4
1 | 2

Laissez-faire

State Level Licensing, e.g., health professionals

Local Better Business Bureaus, Auditors (AICPA)

Government Responsibility

Industry Responsibility

High

None to Low

None to Low

High

serve to avert a crisis or decline of a profession. Survey results showed that 115 organizations cited the need to change image as a major motivation; 52 organizations noted that the motive was a reaction to a previous lack of self-policing.

A third rationale for self-regulation is that the industry or profession can do it better, at less cost, and in a more appropriate fashion than government. In many cases, such as the certification of cosmetologists and real estate appraisers, or the policing of recruiting practices in collegiate athletics (NCAA), the government would rather have the industry do its own standards setting.

In the current climate of environmental complexity, technological change, professional specialization, media scrutiny, and pressure for reduced government spending, carefully designed and managed self-regulation by an industry or profession can serve as a useful institutional alternative for addressing some forms of unwanted business and professional behavior. Given that the complex nature of many new standards requires business and professional expertise, more systematic opportunities are being created for industry associations and professional societies to be involved. Industry and professional self-regulation is one of these. In fact, the trend toward association involvement and government interest in this area is evident in

- current efforts to create self-regulatory systems for mutual fund advertising, all-terrain vehicles (ATVs), recombinant DNA research, computer software, and chain saw safety;

- the reissuance of OMB Circular No. A-119, which encourages federal agency promotion of voluntary standard-setting organizations;

- the activity within the Environmental Protection Agency and the chemical industry for a corporate environmental audit program wherein corporations manage and monitor their own programs; and

- cooperation between the Food and Drug Administration and the Pharmaceutical Manufactures Association (PMA), Washington, D.C., in creating new drug testing standards that meet safety and timeliness criteria.

Even the popular press has offered ideas on those areas where self-regulation demonstrates promise or ignites controversy. Consider the following examples:

- The Professional Golfers Association (PGA), Boca Raton, Florida, feels the groove design on Ping golf clubs offers unfair advantage to users and they have been barred from use on the professional circuit. This issue has not been resolved.

- Following incidents involving some fraternities and sororities, the National Interfraternity Council developed a policy on college campuses to discourage alcohol abuse and underage drinking. It promotes alcohol-free parties.

- A dramatic growth in massage therapy for stress reduction and injury recovery for elite athletes, weekend tennis players, and those in high stress jobs. Since 1983, the field has grown from 1,500 to 7,200 certified therapists; 56 schools now offer training, up from 30 just seven years ago.

- Following the Jim Bakker and Jimmy Swaggart scandals, television evangelists developed a code for ethical fund-raising and funds management.

To determine why self-regulation was developed for their industry or profession, the following question was posed: What motivated or influenced the development of your self-regulation program? Table 2 shows the results.

Of the 252 organizations surveyed, 115 (45.6 percent) developed a program because of the need to change the image of the industry or profession; one in five programs was developed because of a failure of industry to police itself; 29 programs were motivated in response to a threat of government intervention.

For an industry or profession concerned about image, self-regulation provides an opportunity to reshape public opinion. In some cases, survival of a profession may be at stake (television evangelists); in others, it may be a way to bring together a diffuse and differentiated profession around a common set of guidelines or principles (financial planners, direct salespersons).

In general, industry self-regulation operates on the premise that the transaction costs of designing, securing government approval, and operating a system for self-control are less than if government imposes control externally. The presence of a bona fide self-regulatory system signifies that at some level both government and

Table 2. Motivation to Self-Regulate

Most Important No. %	Very Important No. %	Motivation
115 45.6%	23 9.1%	Need to change the image of industry/profession
52 20.6%	21 8.3%	Failure of industry/profession to adequately police itself
29 11.5%	15 6%	Threat of government regulation
17 6.7%	9 3.6%	Consumer pressure
13 5.2%	3 1.2%	Request by government to develop a program
91 36.1%	3 1.2%	Other (e.g., membership request goal of association/leadership; lawyers suggested it; board demand)

NOTE: These results are based on 252 organizations surveyed. Respondents could check off all of the reasons that applied to them.

industry recognize their shared responsibility to address problems and issues without resorting to lengthy court battles. Additionally, it shows that with necessary checks, industry competitors can collaborate on quality standards and other rules of competition without unfair restrictions of trade.

In the technical and administrative standards areas, it could be argued that the fundamental motivation for self-regulation is *economic*. Economic benefit is realized in two ways. First, improved minimum standards for product quality and part interchangeability can expand the overall market for an industry's products. This has the potential for improving revenues at a minimal cost to individual firms within the industry. Second, cost savings may be realized through the joint testing of products, the shared assessment of the costs and benefits of standards under consideration, and/or the time savings realized by minimizing the delays and red tape of government intervention.

Beyond the motivation of cost savings, the mere *threat* of greater government intervention may inspire action. This threat may be averted by self-policing if the industry's standards result in a smaller expected loss of profit. The perception of greater flexibility in the form of response alternatives may also encourage action prior to a government mandate.

Another factor that influences movement toward self-imposed rule making is the actual *directive* to do so from a government body. The SEC's grant of authority to the Accounting Principles Board (APB) and subsequently FASB in the accounting industry is an example.

Identification by individuals within an industry to a professional discipline may also encourage self-control. The obvious examples are the American Medical Association (AMA), Chicago, Illinois, and the American Bar Association (ABA), Chicago, Illinois. Less obvious examples are activities of engineering and scientific societies in the automotive, computer, drug, and aerospace industries. A final motivation for self-regulation is *pressure from nongovernment stakeholders* such as consumers, suppliers, investors and employees.

How Many Self-Regulation Programs Exist?

A dramatic finding of the study is the vast array of different forms of self-policing imposed by industry groups and professions. Respondents were asked the following question: Which categories would you use to describe your self-regulation program? The responses were distributed as follows:

- 59 answered "Technical product, material, or procedure standards";

- 26 answered "Testing and certification of products or materials";

- 121 answered "Certification of individuals";

- 71 answered "Accreditation";

- 123 answered "Enforceable code of business or professional conduct";

- 44 answered "Arbitration/dispute resolution";

- 19 answered "Licensing";

- 36 answered "Other (for example, certify facilities, consumer protection)."

The results show that 252 organizations are responsible for the design and administration of 499 programs. From the data, a number of observations are possible.

First, a number of associations serve as umbrella associations wherein they administer multiple self-regulating programs. Two such associations and their activities are described below:

- The Committee on Allied Health Education and Accreditation (CAHEA) of the American Medical Association serves as a type of nongovernmental umbrella organization for voluntary accreditation activities. CAHEA accredits educational programs in 23 allied health occupational areas in collaboration with 16 review committees—sponsored by 39 national allied health profession organizations and medical specialty societies—as participants in the accreditation process.

- The American National Standards Institute (ANSI) coordinates voluntary standards activities in the United States (more than

10,000 technical standards) and approves national standards. ANSI serves as the United States member of ISO and IEC—the International Organization for Standardization and the International Electrotechnical Commission—provides forums for government-industry cooperation, and is the clearinghouse and central source for information on national and international standards.

The study shows that codes of conduct and certification programs are the most frequently occurring programs. Accreditation accounted for 71 programs in the survey. The two types of technical standards for products and material design and testing comprised a total of 85 programs.

Table 3 offers a more complete listing of program types with illustrative examples. Two important caveats are critical here. First, a wide array of technical standards are well-documented by ANSI and the National Bureau of Standards at the Department of Commerce. Second, while professional codes are well-documented, corporate codes of conduct are not represented in the study. The Ethics Resource Center in Washington serves as a clearinghouse for corporate codes.

What Roles do Associations Play in Self-Regulation?

In many respects, associations and professional societies take on quasi-governmental roles in rule making (legislative), administration and monitoring (executive), and enforcement (judicial) activities. In self-regulation, the process of generating support for a program from industry members and government regulators requires collaboration. The most frequently mentioned activity regarding self-regulation was generating awareness and support for a program among members. The primary responsibility for formulation and enforcement of regulatory standards rests with an industry self-regulatory body (association) rather than a government agency.

Over 60 percent of the organizations highlighted rule making, rule amending, and designing due process procedures as critical. An ongoing, problem-solving relationship exists between the regulatory agency and the industry self-regulating body. If appropriate, a government regulator can perform an oversight role, may share monitoring and enforcement responsibilities, and can threaten to impose more severe direct regulation should self-regulation prove ineffective. Codes are usually voluntary (68.7 percent), and although they are not explicit legal requirements, many are treated as such by the industry. Nonmembers participated in over 50 percent of the programs.

The questionnaire posed a range of questions about the roles and responsibilities associations took on to develop and administer their programs. Table 4 summarizes the results. By far the most prevalent association activities in developing support for self-regulation fall into the categories of (1) membership awareness and support, (2) designing rules and rule-making systems and procedures, and (3) developing appropriate policies for enforcement. Associations use others for ideas and counsel, and, after applying internal procedures to a case, are not remiss to refer it to government. Finally, some associations are willing to create a new organization (14.7 percent) to carry out self-regulatory activities.

In general, an industry self-regulatory system is characterized by rule-making/standard-setting, monitoring, and enforcement stages. Committees within industry associations or professional societies propose standards and may request government approval through advisory opinions. This was done by 40 organizations. Not only do interaction and negotiation help secure approval, but also they can protect the industry from overzealous antitrust claims. Self-regulatory programs are highly adaptive. Over 70 percent of the respondents have changed or amended their programs since their inception. Changes cover such areas as rules, board structure, internal governance, procedures, guidelines, and sanctions.

Monitoring responsibilities clearly do not fall on the association alone. A wide range of stakeholders are involved in the process as suggested in Table 5.

Clearly, while association staff, industry, and professional peers play a large part, other groups including outsiders such as consumers and government agencies are involved. It appears that monitoring and enforcement responsibilities are set up to encourage problem resolution within the self-regulatory system before referring the case to government. Often, government serves as the enforcer of last resort.

Despite antitrust concerns, enforcement is taken seriously. Of those organizations surveyed, 95 of the 252 (38 percent) have sanctioned their members. Sanctions vary widely as shown in Table 6.

Table 3. Examples of Self-Regulatory Standards, Supporting Organizations, and Government Agencies

Types of Self-Regulatory Standards	How Many	Examples	Associations, Professional Groups, and Other Organizations	Representative Government Agencies
Governance		Corporate governance, board of director responsibility	Business roundtable	Justice Department
Ethical principles/codes of conduct	123	Corporate codes of conduct Professional codes of conduct, e.g., brokers, lawyers, doctors, direct salespersons, bill collectors	Corporations, e.g., Johnson & Johnson, Proctor & Gamble Direct Selling Association, American Collectors Association	Federal Trade Commission (FTC)
Institutional Accountability		Performance standards for high school grads in math; revised financing arrangements for hospitals and school systems	State-level business roundtables, High Tech Council, Chicago United	State and local governments
Arbitration/dispute resolution	44	Commercial and labor disputes	American Arbitration Association	
Disclosure, consumer protection	4	Motion pictures, financial performance, fair advertising	Motion Picture Association, Financial Accounting Standards Board	State attorneys general, FTC

Table 3. Examples of Self-Regulatory Standards, Supporting Organizations, and Government Agencies (cont.)

Types of Self-Regulatory Standards	How Many	Examples	Associations, Professional Groups, and Other Organizations	Representative Government Agencies
Licensing	19	Securities dealers, lawyers doctors, hairdressers, and cosmetologists	National Association of Securities Dealers, state bar associations	SEC, state licensing boards
Accreditation	71	Schools, laboratories	Proprietary Schools Association, nursing homes	FTC, state health departments
Certification of individuals/facilities	121	Financial planners, financial analysts, actuaries, chartered life underwriters, accountants, various medical specialists, animal shelters	College for Financial Planning, AICPA, American Humane Association	
Testing materials	26	Toys, kerosene heaters	Toy manufacturers association, Underwriters Laboratories	Department of Commerce
Technical standards: safety, procedures, design/process, labeling	59	Fire inspections, laboratory procedures, animal breeding; process for wood preserving; plywood dimensions; air conditioners, "white goods," and energy use	National Fire Protection Association, American National Standards Institute, Society of American Wood Preservers, plywood manufacturing associations, National Association of Railroads, Association of Home Appliance Manufacturers	EPA, Consumer Product Safety Commission (CPSC), FDA

Table 4. Association Activities in Developing and Administering Self-Regulation Programs

Number	Percent	Activity
197	78.2%	Increase awareness to membership about need for self-regulation
192	76.2%	Form committee to develop rules
191	75.8%	Set rules
178	70.6%	Amend rates
164	65%	Identify need for self-regulation
150	59.5%	Design due process procedures for hearing cases
140	55.6%	Hire legal counsel
140	55.6%	Contact other associations about self-regulatory programs
133	52.8%	Enforce rules
132	52.4%	Sanction individual/firms if rules are violated
115	45.6%	Refer violations to appropriate internal committees
105	41.7%	Develop and maintain contacts with government officials
102	40.5%	Monitor compliance
100	39.7%	Develop tests (if applicable)
77	30.6%	Conduct research of self-regulation programs in related cases
53	21%	Contract out testing (if applicable)
40	15.9%	Seek advisory opinion from government
36	14.7%	Create new organizations to handle self-regulation activities
31	12.3%	Refer violations to appropriate governmental agency
25	9.9%	Other activities

Table 5. Those Responsible for Self-Regulatory Programs

Number	Percent	Who Monitors Compliance
121	48%	Professional association staff
102	40.5%	Association volunteers
102	40.5%	Professional peers
83	32.9%	Individual professions
66	26.2%	Industry peers
57	22.6%	Individual firms
48	19%	Consumers
33	13.1%	Others, e.g., stakeholders, competitors
22	8.7%	Government agencies

Table 6. Enforcement Sanctions

Number	Percent	Sanction
130	51.6%	Private admonition and reprimand
119	47.2%	Suspension or termination of association membership license to practice
84	33.3%	Suspension or termination of use of, or reference to, trademarks insignia
53	21.0%	Other, e.g., warnings, notices
52	20.6%	Public admonition and reprimand
33	13.1%	Referral to government agency
22	8.7%	Monetary fine

How Effective Are Self-Regulation Programs?

For the effort and cost expended, do self-regulation programs really work? This is a difficult question to answer directly. As with traditional regulation by government, associations set minimum guidelines on what should be expected on process issues such as fairness, representation, due process procedures, and success at sanctioning violators of rules. Yet, clear examples of the failure of a system are evident from news stories of safety violations in commercial airplanes, insider trading scandals of stock and options brokers, and inflated property valuations by licensed real estate appraisers. In every profession, however, hundreds, even thousands, of fair and successful transactions may occur daily; one remembers the one or two events where an individual acted improperly. A well-designed system should catch and punish that individual or firm.

A critical measure of effectiveness is the extent to which the program met its goal or purpose. Also, one can look at *how* effectiveness is measured and whether insiders and outsiders are involved. Table 7 summarizes the responses to the following survey question: What measure do you use to judge the effectiveness of your self-regulation program? Nineteen percent of the respondents use no measure of effectiveness. Many use multiple indicators as evidence that their program is working. Tracking complaints from customers and other stakeholders was reported most frequently. External expert evaluations are used in 23 percent of the cases, and public opinion is used in 24 percent. Lack of pressure from government was mentioned in 50 cases. Positive testimonials from both insiders and outsiders were also tracked. At the extreme, law suits against members were noted in nine percent of the cases.

On the question of self-rating, less than 10 percent of the respondents chose not to rate themselves. About 34.5 percent felt their efforts were extremely effective, and 8.2 percent considered their program ineffective. Overall, 149 or 59 percent rated themselves effective. A few open-ended responses were noted in the margins on this item. One association director summed it up quite well. "I used to think being effective at self-regulation would mean reducing complaints by consumers and keeping my members happy. Yet, I have come to realize now that our program is more widely

Table 7. Measures of Effectiveness

Number	Percent	Measure
103	40.8%	Complaints received
70	27.8%	Other, e.g., positive testimonials, cooperation with government agencies
61	24.2%	Public opinion
57	22.6%	External evaluations
50	19.8%	Lack of pressure from government regulators
48	19%	None
33	13.1%	Reports by consumer groups
23	9.1%	Suits filed against members

known, that consumer complaints still come in and some of my members see me as a watchdog. I know, however, that we're doing a good job. You have to commit to this role, which runs against the grain of our traditional 'old boys' club."

What Are the Necessary and Sufficient Conditions for Success?

From the combined analysis thus far, it appears that the following factors are the most critical in explaining initial approval and ongoing success of a self-regulatory system:

- The association, via members or key individuals, must *recognize the need* for self-regulation. The ability to convince others in associations and government of the need is also vital.

- The association or professional society must have the *capacity* for self-regulation. This includes financial resources, staffing, and membership interest. In some cases, this capacity is added or developed because of the commitment to taking on the self-regulatory role.

- An *individual leader or champion* appears to play a pivotal role. The individual embodies the cause and serves as a technical resource, political scout, committee member, and liaison in the network.

- The *structure* (legal and organizational) is key. Antitrust concerns are real and must be carefully considered in the design, organization, and administration of a program.

In general, the better programs are

- formed on a specific set of issues,

- adaptable and responsive to new issues and concerns,

- supported by members and have a track record of success built over time,

- willing to address the tough issues and "go to the mat" if needed,

- endorsed by government (if appropriate) via advisory opinion or other form of approval or legitimacy.

Critical Current Issues in Self-Regulation

In the final section of the survey, we allowed respondents to offer their perspective on the current needs and issues they faced in managing their self-regulation programs. It is clear that promoting a better image to the external public and within their own industry was recognized as an issue. This parallels the earlier finding that the major motivation for self-regulation was the need to improve the image of an industry or profession.

Legal issues regarding antitrust and product or practice liability were noted by many organizations. Proper counsel in the design, approval, and operation of a system is mandatory, yet it does not guarantee that the system or procedure will go unchallenged. Chances are a challenge will occur, and the best protection will be a well-designed code with appropriate due process procedures.

About 55 of the organizations surveyed are concerned about further government intervention, 21 see a need for more liaison with government, and 44 are concerned about staffing issues. Clearly, opportunities exist for ASAE and other organizations (legal, public relations, and others) to provide technical assistance, education, and legal advice on these issues.

Chapter 4

Guidelines for Developing a Self-Regulation Program

Ideas and suggestions for developing a self-regulation program are based on the experiences of association executives and lawyers. Two themes are reinforced here. First, do not seriously consider a self-regulation program without involving legal counsel familiar with this area. Second, recognize that the process of self-regulation requires an ongoing commitment to developing rules, making improvements, and utilizing processes that insure fairness, professionalism, and customer/client service. When these criteria upset association members or fractionalize the association, even the most visionary association executive may feel challenged. The conflict can be managed. In some cases, the creative tension may be good for the organization because it encourages dialogue and an examination of the organization's purposes and values. If self-regulation is the right thing to do and in the broader interest of the association's constituents, it should serve the membership as well as the public.

Getting Started

The research study showed that the following conditions catalyze the development of self-regulation.

Motivation for Cooperative Action. Given awareness of a problem (need for a standard), the industry must perceive that a self-imposed standard has the potential for a reasonably distributed economic benefit without changing the competitive structure of the industry or threatening any firm's distinctive competence. Avoidance of unnecessary stringency is potentially as important as other economic gains.

Available Organized Outside Support. Trade associations and professional societies play a critical roles in organizing self-regulation activities. Independence and professional management are vital to engendering commitment. Communication and control systems between these organizations and government are critical.

The Establishment of a Means for Monitoring and Enforcing Standards. A variety of examples of alternative monitoring and enforcement methods involving industry, government, consumer panels, and outside consultants are prevalent. The form these activities take is not as critical as their potential effectiveness. Avoidance of potential conflict of interest needs to be balanced with the cost of duplication of effort. Again, the trade associations and professional societies can play a role in establishing the balance. Government's role should focus on how to manage this part of the regulatory process.

It is worth repeating here that the better programs are

- formed on a specific set of issues,

- adaptable and responsive to new issues and concerns,

- supported by members and have a track record of success built over time,

- willing to address the tough issues and "go to the mat" if needed, and

- endorsed by government (if appropriate) via advisory opinion or their form of approval or legitimacy.

With these ideas in mind, consider the following roles associations take on in the self-regulation process: educating the association and the public, rule making, monitoring, and enforcement. A description of the activities associated with these roles is shown as a checklist in Table 8. Table 9 shows how various associations have structured their self-regulatory systems.

Education of Association Members and Constituents

Educating members and other constituencies is a critical role for association executives involved in self-regulation. Beyond recognizing and convincing others of the need for self-regulation, education entails the ongoing process of providing information to those who need it—even after a self-regulation program is designed and approved, the association executive must keep all parties informed about the issues, concerns, and challenges to the program.

The following elements of this educational role are suggested from the survey results. First, the association, via key individuals, must *recognize the need* for self-regulation. Having a handful of supporters is not enough. The ability to convince other parties via thoughtful discussion and description is vital. In many ways, this groundwork establishes the preconditions needed for self-regulation to take place.

Second, the association or professional society must have the *capacity* for self-regulation. This includes financial resources, staffing, and membership interest. In some cases, this capacity is added or developed because of the commitment to taking on the self-regulatory role. This is both a financial and human resource issue.

Third, an *individual leader or champion* appears to play a pivotal role. The individual embodies the cause and serves as a technical resource, political scout, committee member, and liaison in the network. The champion is the chief educator or coach for the program.

Fourth, the *structure* (legal and organizational) is key. Antitrust concerns are real and must be carefully considered in the design, organization, and administration of a program. The structure should embody characteristics of a learning organization—systems view, adaptability, information openness, and personal growth. In general, the association executive should

- be prepared to explain the self-regulation program—its rationale, procedures, and structure;

- publicize the program;

- educate members, customers, government agencies, and professionals; and

- explain values to all constituencies via brochures, news releases and word of mouth.

Rule Making

The real test of an organization's commitment to self-regulation

Table 8. A Checklist of Activities Associated with Self-Regulation

Education of Association Members and Constituents

Identify the need for a program.
Be prepared to explain program rationale, procedures, structures.
Publicize the program.
Educate members, customers, government agencies, and professionals.
Explain value to all constituencies via brochures, news releases, word of mouth.
Listen to dissent and discover opportunities for expansion, amendment.

Rule making

Identify the need for a program.
Choose type of program.
Request legal support and advice.
If appropriate, solicit government agency to support via advisory opinion or other approval.
Enroll membership in the process.
Develop rules and rule-making process.
Design preliminary program with rule-making, monitoring, and enforcement components and structure for carrying out the process; if appropriate, identify a partner organization to share responsibilities.

Monitoring

Install procedures for monitoring behavior, e.g., handling complaints.
Include due process safeguards.
Keep informed about activities in your industry.
Update program or code when necessary.
Maintain detailed records, e.g., meeting minutes, complaints, written correspondence.

Enforcement

Design appropriate penalties. Be watchful of antitrust concerns.
Bring legal counsel on board to support any enforcement action.
Use due process procedures to enforce rules as necessary.
Utilize government as an enforcer of last resort.
Attempt to handle the issue internally before going public.

Table 9. Examples of Self-Regulation Roles Undertaken by Associations

ROLES: activities, examples	Advertising via American Advertising Federation, NARB/CBB†	Financial Disclosures via AICPA	Securities trading via NASD	Home appliance via AHAM
INFLUENCE: increase awareness; identify problem	saw need to take action			identify need to take action
change rules, seek advisory opinion	sought advisory opinion, collaborated with FTC	SEC request	SEC request in 1930s	
create new organization	NAD*/ NARB link with CBB	APB, FASB	NASD	U. Labs, ASTM
publicize program	in industry	to public	to public	to public
MAKE RULES: develop committee	reps of major firms	major firms and stakeholders		major appliance consumer action panel
design program substance			licensing and codes of conduct	performance specifications and labeling
procedure to amend rules			yes	
CARRY OUT RULES: testing		audits	license exam for traders	
review	use industry and third-party reps	yes, peer review	the exchanges	
sanctions, government oversight	yes, with FTC oversight	no before 1987; yes after 1987	yes, with SEC oversight	

† National Advertising Review Board/Council of Better Business Bureaus
* National Advertising Division

Table 9. Examples of Self-Regulation Roles Undertaken by Associations (cont.)

ROLES: activities, examples	Direct selling via Direct Selling Association	Infant formula via INFACT	Motion Picture Association	Van conversions
INFLUENCE: increase awareness; identify problem	took action on "image problem"	letters to Nestles	parents' concerns about movie content	fire hazards, safety
change rules, seek advisory opinion	developed relationship w/FTC, proposed code	influence public opinion, boycott		
create new organization	third-party code administrator		motion picture ratings council	via conversion manufacturing association
publicize program	to consumers	via letters to editors	to public	via manufacturing and public
MAKE RULES: develop committee	major firms	stakeholders	via theatre operators	reps of firms
design program substance	consumer code of conduct	World Health Organization marketing practices code	ratings systems	design and material specifications
procedure to amend rules	yes			yes
CARRY OUT RULES: testing			use public opinion	certification
review	independent code administration	Nestle Audit Commission	labels and signage	
sanctions, government oversight	yes, with FTC oversight		no	yes, take away seal

occurs at the rule-making stage. The need for a program, much less its rigor, may not be well understood by members, government officials, or other parties. Doing things right the first time is critical.

The primary responsibility for the formulation and enforcement of regulatory standards rests with an industry self-regulatory body (association) rather than a government agency. The process of generating and maintaining support for a self-regulation program from industry members and government regulators requires collaboration. A close relationship usually exists between the regulatory agency, the industry self-regulating body, and the industry participants. Typically, government performs a vigilance role, and may share monitoring and enforcement responsibilities; government can threaten to impose more severe direct regulation should self-regulation prove ineffective. Typically, product standards and credentialing requirements are mandatory, while codes of conduct are usually voluntary. Although these codes are not explicit legal requirements, many are treated as such by the industry when sanctioning inappropriate behavior.

In general, the rule-making roles are to

- identify the need for a program,

- choose the type of program,

- request legal support and advice,

- design the preliminary program with rule-making, monitoring, and enforcement components and a structure for carrying out the process; if appropriate, identify a partner organization to share responsibilities,

- enroll membership in the process,

- solicit government agency support via advisory opinion or other approval, if appropriate,

- develop rules and the rule-making process, and

- create a separate organization to handle the program, if appropriate.

Note the importance of soliciting legal advice on the specific design of a program. Use other association's programs as preliminary models. Consider the entire program (rules, monitoring, and enforcement) from the early stages. Having a well-designed package of rules and procedures will be necessary to generate member support and government approval. Wherever possible, secure support of related organizations (testing houses, related associations, other constituencies). If necessary, consider creating and using a separate third-party organization to manage the self-regulation process. This avoids possible conflicts with members over pending decisions or cases. Keep constituencies (members, staff, government officials, others) informed of your progress, time frame, and game plan.

Monitoring

This role entails the ongoing observation of behaviors and competencies, the handling of issues, and the managing of complaints or exemptions to normal operating procedures. While much of it is procedural once the system is designed and tested, the monitoring role is one area where organizations have identified needed amendments and changes to their systems.

In general, associations should

- install procedures for monitoring behavior such as handling complaints, recognizing failures, and correcting mistakes;

- include due process safeguards;

- keep informed about activities, pressures, and trends in the industry;

- update the program or code when necessary; and

- maintain detailed records.

The association must be careful to incorporate due process procedures into the system. The minimum requirements to meet elementary due process safeguards suggested by Braemer (1969) include

- reasonable notice of the charges against the member;

- fair notice of the hearing upon the member;

- a fair opportunity to hear the evidence and confront and cross-examine witnesses against the member;

- a fair opportunity to refute the charges against the member; and

- a hearing before an unbiased tribunal.

Enforcement

Enforcement is the most problematic from both legal and managerial viewpoints. Since most codes and standards are voluntary, enforcement of a rule may be difficult. Additionally, if the enforcement process involves a sanction that restrains trade (for example, taking someone's license away), the program may violate an antitrust rule. Managerially, the enforcement role is difficult. Even when necessary, sanctioning an association member can require a choice among personal friendships, memberships, interests, and professional duty. Using the third-party organization to handle such issues helps insulate the association executive from this conflict. Two suggestions repeated by numerous survey respondents were: (1) strive to handle the conflict internally before going public, and (2) when necessary, use government as the enforcer of last resort.

The enforcement activities could be summarized as follows:

- design appropriate penalties and be watchful of antitrust concerns;

- bring legal counsel on board to support any enforcement action;

- use due process procedures to enforce rules as necessary;

- utilize government as an enforcer of last resort; and

- attempt to handle the issue internally before going public.

Chapter 5

The Direct Selling Association Code of Conduct: A Case Study

The development and operation of a self-regulatory system in the direct sales industry illustrates the collaborative process in securing industry support and in working with government regulators. This section presents the history of the self-regulation program via the code of ethics in the direct selling industry. It begins with a description of the setting at the time the code was considered and discusses the activities of the Direct Selling Association (DSA), Washington, D.C., in developing, approving, and using the code.

Research Methods

Developing the detailed case study on the Direct Selling Association Code of Conduct entailed the use of the following data-gathering methods:

- personal interviews with principal actors in the code development process as well as with current administrators and staff at the DSA;

- personal interviews with informal observers of the code in operation, including a White House staff member from the Office of Consumer Affairs, the executive director of the Ethics Resource Center, and the executive director of the Council of Better Business Bureaus who administers a self-regulation program for the advertising industry;

- a collection of archival information including meeting minutes, brochures, internal memoranda, and reports;

- review of articles written about the DSA code;

- use of library resources for industry analysis and biographical sketches.

The Direct Selling Industry

In general terms, the direct selling industry comprises those firms which sell their products and services via door-to-door or in-the-home sales. Just over 800 firms make up this $8.5 billion industry. Major firms include such household names as Avon, Mary Kay Cosmetics, Amway, Fuller Brush, Tupperware, World Book Encyclopedia, and Shaklee. The 135 member firms in the Direct Selling Association have sales of about $7.5 billion. One large company, Tupperware, is not a member of the association.

Historically, the major products sold door-to-door have included cosmetics, pots and pans, brushes and combs, encyclopedias, and food containers. More recently, products such as clothing, home decor, jewelry, bedroom fashions, and sexual aids are being sold in home sales demonstrations.

For a short period in the 1970s, direct selling companies were take-over candidates. General Foods owned Vivian Woodward, a cosmetics direct marketer, and Consolidated Foods held Fuller Brush. Both sold off these companies because of poor performance (Holland 1980).

According to Holland (1980), three methods of direct selling are common:

1. Door-to-door selling is used by some companies like Avon. Generally, the sales representative is assigned a particular area and seeks customers by going from house to house.

2. The party plan (Mary Kay uses this method) is becoming more popular in cosmetics. The sales representative makes a presentation to a group of potential customers who have expressed their interest by attending a demonstration party.

3. A third method involves the placing of catalog orders by customers. The orders are delivered in person by a sales representative, who solicits other orders.

Using a variation of Porter's (1980) model of industry analysis, shown in Figure 2, the industry's commonality in home sales provides a picture of the pressures it faces from various sources. In

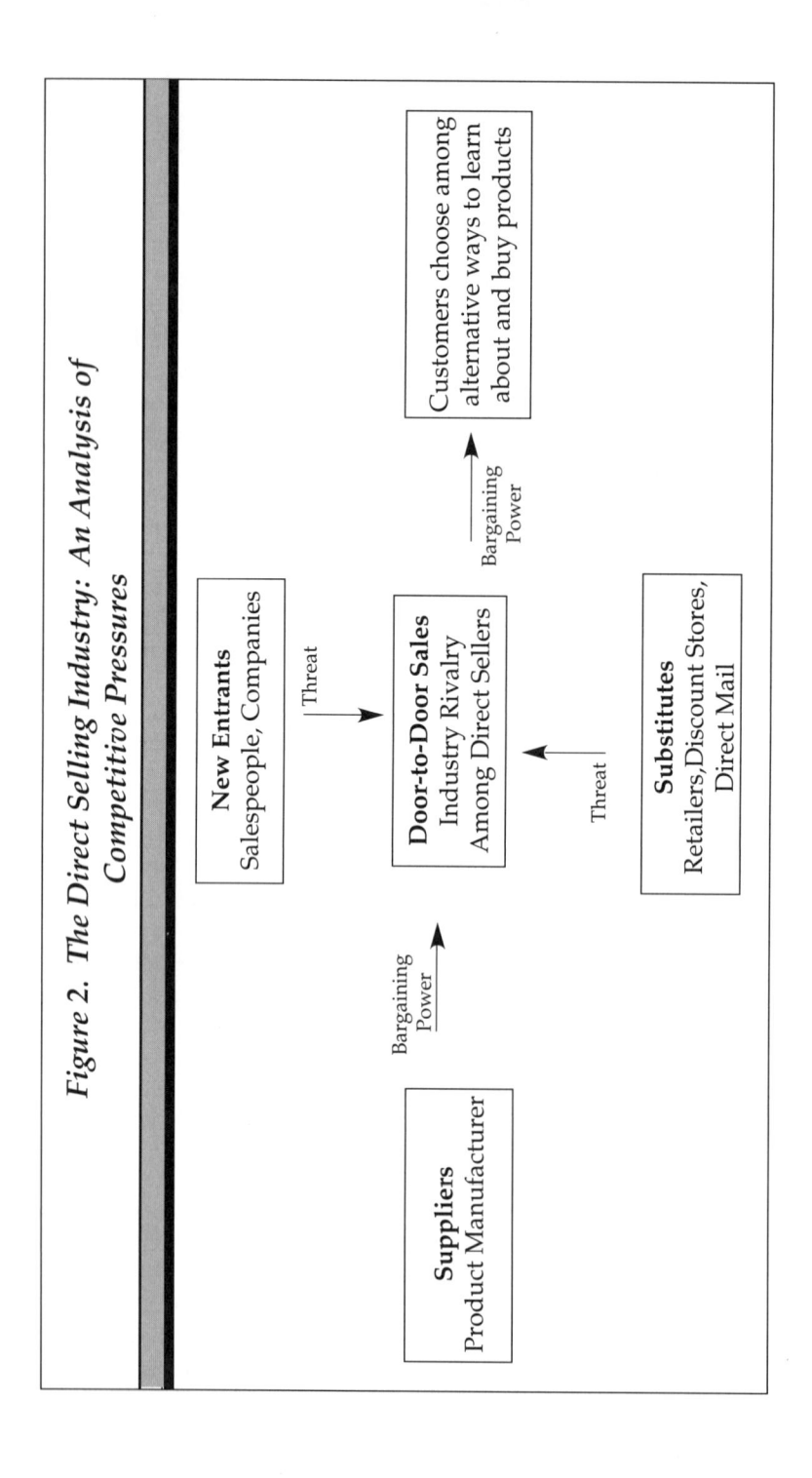

Figure 2. The Direct Selling Industry: An Analysis of Competitive Pressures

New Entrants
Salespeople, Companies

↓ Threat

Suppliers
Product Manufacturer

Bargaining Power →

Door-to-Door Sales
Industry Rivalry Among Direct Sellers

Bargaining Power →

Customers choose among alternative ways to learn about and buy products

← Threat

Substitutes
Retailers, Discount Stores, Direct Mail

many cases, the companies are vertically integrated into supplying their own products (for example, Amway, Avon, Mary Kay and Shaklee), thus reducing or eliminating supplier bargaining power. New entrants come in two forms: (1) new salespeople can choose to join the organization and compete for territory or customers; and (2) new companies can emerge to sell the same products. This second form is the most prevalent in door-to-door sales of cosmetics. Substitutes are the alternative ways similar products might be sold and these substitutes include retail stores, discounters, and direct mail. With each of these methods, customers or buyers have control over the purchase decision. A buyer can shop in retail stores or quietly peruse a direct mail catalog with little or no interaction with a salesperson. With direct selling, a buyer must choose to let someone into her or his home.

To be competitive, direct salespersons must be able to solicit for leads and gain entrance into individuals' homes to present a sales pitch. Perceptions are critical. A poor reputation, a bad image created by fly-by-night operators, or anecdotal stories about pressure tactics could spell disaster for all direct sellers. People may refuse to open their doors and local jurisdictions may threaten to ban door-to-door solicitation entirely. Because of these threats to the very essence of the direct selling method, the industry moved to consider self-regulation.

The Pressures: An Industry in Crisis

The 1950s and 1960s were characterized by unprecedented economic growth, particularly in the consumer goods industries. This growth led to refinement and expansion of alternative marketing approaches—upscale and discount retailing in suburban shopping malls, direct mail, and door-to-door sales.

A major byproduct of the growing consumer economy was the evolution of a consumer movement. Spurred by Ralph Nader's exposé on the American automobile industry, *Unsafe at Any Speed,* the movement gained political and grass-roots support. The significance of consumer issues was institutionalized by the Johnson administration in the creation of an Office of Consumer Affairs in the White House, and in appointments of consumer advocates to various commissions such as the Federal Trade Commission (FTC) (McGlauclin, June 17, 1984).

In addition to consumerist activities in the late 1960s, environmental and other issue groups succeeded in bringing additional public-interest legislation to Congress. Emerging within a three-year period, from 1968–1971, were such new government entities as the Environmental Protection Agency (EPA), the Occupational Safety and Health Administration (OSHA), the Consumer Product Safety Commission (CPSC), and the National Highway Traffic Safety Administration (NHTSA) (Weidenbaum 1981). In general, government's response to pressure from issue groups during this period was to initiate new regulations and establish organizations to administer them.

State and local governments were also getting involved during these years. State and local offices of consumer affairs were being established to monitor companies engaged in fraudulent practices and to provide a centralized consumer complaint mechanism. The National Association of Consumer Agency Administrators, Trenton, New Jersey, was formed in 1970 to coordinate the activities of the various state consumer agencies and serve as a clearinghouse of information. To control the sporadic but well publicized problems of high-pressure door-to-door sales, some local governments were considering licensing programs. Any direct salesperson would have been required to register with the locality, pay a fee, and carry a picture identification badge. For many direct salespeople who covered large territories, this would have meant numerous registrations, fees, and badges.

In 1969, to counter the pressure tactics of a handful of direct sales forces, the National Consumer Law Center at Boston College proposed a sale affirmation system whereby a customer purchasing a product from a direct salesperson would need to sign and mail in a card to indicate the sale was valid (Offen 1984). Also at this time, the FTC was considering a "cooling off rule" that would allow consumers 48 hours to consider their choice and back out of the purchase if they wished.

For the direct selling industry, general economic growth and the consumerist movement created a threatening dilemma. The industry was expanding rapidly both in terms of individual firm growth and in the expansion of new types of products being sold door-to-door. Yet, the growth of direct sales influenced merchants in some communities to request legislation either banning direct selling or requiring licensing for door-to-door sales forces. In addition, consumer complaints about abuses by fly-by-night operators and pressure tactics from salespeople fueled the fire for a legislative response.

Evolution of the Direct Selling Association

With the pressures from federal, state, and local governments, as well as consumer interests, the leadership of major corporations in the industry (Amway, World Book, and Avon) recognized that some action was needed. Neil Offen, the current DSA president, described the climate in 1969 (1984): "They were sick of the characters that had given the industry a bad name; their pride was affected."

Initially, what kind of action to take was not clear. Doing something individually would not address the problem; many firms already took responsibility for policing their sales forces. A collective response or system was needed to weed out those firms which spoiled the industry's reputation. Yet, simply lobbying as an industry against government interference of any kind, which had historically been the Direct Selling Association's position, was not enough. Proposing a tough self-policing system via a code of ethics had its problems as well. Member firms valued their independence and resisted the idea of third-party intervention (be it government or peers). Of those favorably disposed to the idea, little agreement existed about how strong to make a code. Also, it was not clear whether the relevant government agencies, notably the FTC or local governments, would accept the idea of self-regulation in the industry.

To confound the matter, the Direct Selling Association, located at that time in Winona, Minnesota, was not really suited to organize and coordinate the development of a code system. In existence since 1910, it was, in Offen's (1984) words, "a municipal lobbying and drinking club." With a full-time staff of four and a budget of less than $100,000, there was little knowledge about the ways of Washington and limited experience in mobilizing the membership. The DSA was principally geared to lobby against local ordinances that restricted door-to-door sales. Developing and running a self-regulation system simply was beyond the capacity of this rural Minnesota organization.

Despite various sources of resistance in its membership ranks, the limited capacity of the existing association, and the distance from the political action in Washington, D.C., industry leaders and the DSA recognized that taking some positive action was critical. In 1968 finding new leadership for the association was first priority. J. Robert Brouse, a tough-minded and experienced association executive with a Washington track record, was hired. His first directive was strategic—move the association to Washington, D.C., providing access to key decision makers and establishing the organization's presence in the nation's capital. This move paralleled the opening of Washington, D.C., offices of major corporations during the same time (Mahon 1981). Brouse recognized, as did corporate public affairs officers, that effectively influencing and responding to government actions could best be managed in close proximity to those having the decision-making power.

The Code: Its Development and Legal Context

Having established the Washington, D.C., office, Brouse's long-range program to improve the image of the industry was conceived and initiated. He sought to professionalize the industry via a code of conduct. Aware that window dressing and speeches would not fool the FTC or consumers, he felt a strong code with an enforcement system was essential. His rationale was basic—the code and its system would add a level for customer problem resolution before the problem was presented to government or the media. Before this code, a customer with a complaint (about a salesperson or a product) would first go to the company and then to government or the media to get attention or satisfaction. With the proposed system, an individual not directly affiliated with the association—a professional, independent code administrator—would be responsible for handling a complaint, thereby keeping the media and government out of the issue. This new system would demonstrate the ability of the direct selling industry to keep its own house in order.

To insure that the code did not violate antitrust law and could withstand due process challenges, research to develop the code was extensive. Gerald E. Gilbert, a Washington, D.C., attorney was hired to draft the code. He was experienced at association law and in dealing with the FTC. Few models of codes and self-regulation systems with applicability to direct sales existed. Most formal systems focused on product standards (home appliances), or on licensing (the securities industry). Landmark cases, advisory opinions, and administrative rulings uncovered a question regarding government's (the FTC) resistance to the principle of self-policing. As Gilbert noted in a memo to Brouse in 1972:

One of the major conceptual objections to the establishment of such a program (establishment of a code) was that a private group should not and cannot legally exercise powers that are reserved only for the government. Contrary to private industry, the opponents of industry self-regulation pointed out that the government's actions are subject, substantively and procedurally, to many legal safeguards and restraints.

To insure that a code once approved by the membership would not encounter legal opposition by the FTC, Gilbert looked carefully at advisory opinions of FTC commissioners. In his 1972 memo, Gilbert pointed out:

> One of the main sources (of resistance) was the dissenting statement of Commissioner Elman in the Federal Trade Commission's Advisory Opinion Digest No. 128. That Advisory Opinion concerned a Code of Ethics for the Magazine Publishers' Association which involved a group of producers of products sold by door-to-door salesmen. Obviously, this was very appropriate and germane reference for the Direct Selling Industry. Although a majority vote of the Commission in that opinion sanctioned the adoption of that particular proposal—in part on a trial basis with certain restrictions—Commissioner Elman wrote a strong dissent not only on that particular proposal, but on the establishment of self-regulatory codes in general.

The text of Commissioner Elman's dissent is as follows:

> With the best of intentions, a trade association has proposed, and Commission now approves, the establishment of a code which provides for the exercise of the powers of government of a private group.
>
> It is one thing to encourage businessmen to promote voluntary compliance with the law. It is something else to approve a private scheme of law enforcement, where investigations are conducted by private "policemen" and where violations of privately-decreed "laws" are punished by fines and penalties imposed by private "judges" after privately-conducted "trials."

The Code's Administrator and his staff will apparently function like a small version of the Federal Trade Commission. But there is a big difference between such an administrator and the commission, which is a public agency of government, with powers and duties that are defined and circumscribed by specific statutory provisions enacted by Congress. The decisions and orders of the commission are subject to judicial review. Commission proceedings are public and must be conducted in conformity with the requirements of due process, the Administrative Procedures Act, and other applicable provisions of law. Findings of fact must be supported by substantial evidence on the record. In short, all our actions are subject, substantively and procedurally, to the basic safeguards and restraints established by law.

It is fundamental that the regulatory powers of government are too awesome to be turned over to private policemen, prosecutors, and judges—no matter how well-intentioned. Regulation of business—at least when it involves the imposition of fines and penalties for violations of prescribed standards of conduct—is the job of government agencies and officials bound by the limitations of due process and the rule of law. It runs against the basic grain of American society to permit private "vigilantes" to act as policemen and to allow private judges to hold "kangaroo courts" where punishment is imposed. The fundamental safeguards and restraints which protect the public against arbitrary or lawless official action are absent when the powers of government are sought to be exercised by private individuals or groups. I think the Commission is taking a long step backward in approving the usurpation by a trade association of the law enforcement powers and duties of an agency of government.

In drafting an acceptable code, Elman's statements needed to be taken seriously. In Gilbert's (1972) words: "The code would need to provide for due process, would not impose fines and penalties for violations of prescribed standards of conduct, and yet would have sufficient teeth in it to make such a code meaningful and worthwhile. "

William D. Dixon, former attorney in the Division of Advisory Opinions at the FTC, was consulted unofficially and informally to discuss possible provisions and approaches. To draft the procedural safeguards for the enforcement provisions of the code, the Administrative Procedures Act was reviewed as well.

On completing his research, the drafting of the text and procedures began. In Gilbert's (1972) words:

> The substantive provisions of the Code were drafted in light of the kinds of conduct that has been subject to criticism by the Federal Trade Commission and other state and federal law enforcement agencies. The enforcement procedures were the most difficult to draft from a legal point of view. It was necessary to focus carefully on the degree of any sanction that would be provided by the Code and its impact on the competitive position of an accused because of antitrust implications.

In finalizing the enforcement procedures, Gilbert notes:

> We decided to take the conservative approach and not provide any specific sanctions other than providing simply that unresolved questions of compliance be referred to the appropriate government agency for consideration as a possible violation of law. Before even reaching that point, it was proposed that the procedures provide the same degree of due process safeguards that would normally be required for an expulsion type of enforcement measure. The proposed Code further incorporated the use of an administrator and precautionary provisions that discouraged the role of competitors in the handling of any complaint.

Thus, the DSA protected itself from possible antitrust violations by not specifying sanctions and by incorporating due process procedures into the process. These procedures included verbal attempt at settling an issue, written complaint, informing of accused party, informal hearing, rebuttal, committee review, formal hearing, and appeal. Moreover, they disallowed any competitors from handling a complaint and from using publicity about possible code violations.

While Gilbert was researching and drafting the code, Brouse focused attention on building membership support for the code. He knew membership approval was needed before they could (1) obtain an FTC advisory opinion on the code and system, and (2) publicize the code to the government and the public. This approval was his toughest challenge.

In late 1969, he contacted known opponents to the code, primarily small, "mom-and-pop" direct selling companies, to secure their votes. Their concern was simply a fear of interference by outsiders; they wanted to handle customer complaints by themselves. Some felt they had done nothing wrong, and to agree with the code would suggest they had engaged in pressure selling. The larger companies (Electrolux and some big-ticket companies) opposing the code felt it was too strong. Brouse used a basic argument to counter both sets of concerns—the code and its support system was critical to the survival of direct selling; it represented action to improve the industry's image; and it focused on consumer protection, not intra-industry rivalry, to address deception.

At the spring 1970 meeting of the DSA membership, the proposed code was presented and discussed at length. Even with Brouse's efforts, two clear factions representing extreme positions were evident. On the one hand, the dissenters (some smaller companies, Electrolux, and some big-ticket companies) were against a code with teeth. They felt firms should police themselves internally and not be subject to outside scrutiny and review. If any code was to be adopted at all, they wanted it to be aspirational only.

On the other hand, supporters of the code wanted stricter sanctions and rules to deal with consumer abuse. Comprising many of the larger and national firms (Amway, Avon, World Book), they felt the code system was the way to rid the industry of fly-by-night operators.

A heated debate lasted over an hour during the business meeting. Each side postured itself with ideological views for and against the code. The proponents won out on a simple majority vote, 43 to 30, by convincing some smaller companies that the code would help them.

The acceptance of the code marked the first example of a consumer code. As Offen (1976) wrote:

> The DSA code of ethics is strictly a consumer protection code. The net effect of its implementation is to make restitution to consumers who have been mistreated and, thereby, make it more difficult for charlatans to deceive the public. Naturally, this results in improving the climate of business for legitimate merchants and helps promote competition in a fair and nondeceptive manner. Free and open competition is, therefore, fostered by the code and it is not used, as perhaps some

codes are, as a subterfuge for price fixing or other anticompetitive acts or practices.

Because of its careful preparation and Gilbert's ongoing contact with the FTC, an FTC advisory opinion providing government's stamp of approval was made in late 1970, about five months after membership acceptance.

The Code and Its System

The code, in contrast to many aspirational statements of principles, is a regulatory code. It provides rules regarding product offerings, terms of sale, warranties, and guarantees; it prohibits pyramid schemes. The code provides for monitoring and settling consumer complaints through an independent code administrator who is retained by the DSA board of directors.

In addition to the code itself, the association provides a set of action guidelines (as a brochure) for members to follow. In general, it notes member company requirements for code compliance, including checking company sales documents, training company representatives, reviewing company marketing plans, and investigating and resolving customer complaints. The brochure also indicates procedures to follow in the event of a customer complaint. A five-step procedure is possible, though most problems are handled with Steps 1 and 2. The steps include:

Step 1. Complaint is received in writing; the complaint is forwarded to the accused party; an informal investigation begins.

Step 2. An informal hearing is called and conducted; the administrator's preliminary decision is delivered.

Step 3. An opportunity is provided for company rebuttal; an appeal for special ethics committee review can be made.

Step 4. Members of the special ethics committee are appointed; positions by administrator and accused company are submitted; a formal hearing date (minimum 30 days' notice) is selected; a formal hearing is held and a decision is made.

Step 5. If the company is found guilty and fails to satisfy the consumer upon instruction of the code administrator, the association can request federal/state authorities to prosecute the member; the industry and public will be informed of association actions.

In the event the code administrator cannot resolve a dispute, the case can be referred to the FTC. To date, of the approximately 600 cases received by the code administrators, no case has taken such a course.

The code is a consumer code as opposed to a professional code of conduct. Only bona fide consumers can file complaints. Salespeople cannot use this system to challenge techniques or practices of other firms nor can they use it to complain about their colleagues. Consumers who have a complaint about a direct salesperson or company typically notify a local or state consumer agency after they receive no satisfaction from direct company contact. Because of the DSA nationwide networking effort with these agencies, staff persons know about the code and can provide customers with the name and number of the current code administrator. In some cases, such as World Book Encyclopedia, member firms include the name of the code administrator in their marketing materials presented at the time of sale. Typically, settlements entail reimbursement for defective or returned products, most of which range in value from $25–$250.

All members of the association are covered by the code. Along with yearly dues payments, presidents of member firms are required to sign a statement on their membership renewal form that certifies they have read, understood, and will abide by the code. As of 1979, a code responsibility officer appointed for each member company must also sign the form. This individual serves as the contact person in the company when the code administrator has a question or problem to address.

In the event a company is found in violation of the code, resignation from the association does not exempt them from code coverage. Since they were a member of the association when the violation occurred, the case is handled using normal procedures.

Adaptation and Evolution: The Code and the Association in Operation

Once the code was approved by the membership and the FTC,

Brouse and key administrator Neil Offen, the DSA legal counsel in 1971, recognized their next concern—how to let consumers know the code existed, and that consumers would have recourse, if necessary. Brochures describing the code and consumer rights were printed and distributed to member companies. According to Offen (1976):

> DSA Vice President of Communications Eileen Creamer O'Neill, who had responsibility for this program, provided actual letters, scripts, press releases, and similar items that the companies could reproduce as their own. She also produced a brochure, "DSA Opens the Door to Consumer Protection," which was published in quantity for internal distribution and for sale to member firms who then could imprint it with their own name, logo, address, and so forth and distribute it to the general public. The first million copies of the brochure were printed under a grant from Avon Products, Inc., and the first company subsequently to make purchases totaling a million copies for dissemination to prospective consumers was the Kirby Company.

In mid-1972, the DSA also engaged in a public education campaign to get its message out. Since the total DSA budget at the time was only $300,000, efforts were limited to one state, Wisconsin, to test methods for consumer communication. On a $25,000 budget and with the support of Wisconsin-based member companies, DSA organized radio and television public service announcements, sent out press releases, and arranged for DSA staff and corporate executives to appear on talk shows. In addition, DSA contacted state legislators, consumer protection groups, chambers of commerce, better business bureaus, extension home economists, and various civic groups (Offen 1976).

What DSA learned from the three-month project was that considerable ongoing effort and money was needed to get its message to the public. In addition, DSA recognized an increase in complaints against those companies which were doing their jobs in communicating with the customer. According to Rogel (1982), most were based on consumer misunderstanding about the code. In the entire first year, only 25 complaints were received. Over the years 1979-1984, an average of 40 complaints were received each year.

Rogel (1984) noted that the nature of complaints falls into three general categories: (1) dissatisfaction with the product and requests for refunds (15–20 yearly); (2) merchandise not delivered (3–6 yearly); and (3) billing problems (10–15 yearly). Most complaints are handled with a phone call or letter to the company. The hardest cases to address are with companies going bankrupt that may not have funds to reimburse customers. Over the last two years, three companies in the industry filed for bankruptcy. Rogel remarked that each is still in the process of trying to make good with their customers. A total of 40 customers are affected, with a total dollar value of approximately $2,000.

One organizational response to lessons learned from the public information campaign was the establishment of a nonprofit Direct Selling Education Foundation. As of 1978, over one-half million dollars were generated from member companies to (1) explain and promote the direct selling industry as a method of retailing, (2) provide tips on what consumers should be wary of in dealing with door-to-door salespersons, and (3) inform aggrieved consumers about where they could go for assistance (Offen 1976).

Change also occurred in the code administrator position during the first seven years. Until 1976, three lawyers had held the post. Since it was a new and highly visible position, one which required administrative and political expertise, the first code administrator was Clarence Lundquist, a respected career civil servant from the Wage and Hour Division of the Department of Labor under Presidents Eisenhower, Kennedy, and Johnson. He served two years. The second code administrator was Ken Roberts, the Democrat from Alabama who was a consumerist and early supporter of Ralph Nader. He brought a more public and external view to the job and served four years before retiring from public life. Serving for less than a year was Henry Robinson, a member of the Small Business Council. In 1979, he was replaced by William Rogel, the current administrator. Mr. Rogel was former deputy director of the Bureau of Consumer Protection at the FTC and legal counsel to the American Advertising Federation (AAF), Washington, D.C. The AAF is known for its well-established self-regulation program with the Better Business Bureau and the National Advertising Review Board.

Administrators are paid on retainer from the DSA board of directors. In 1983, Rogel estimated he spent an average of one day per week on code administrator responsibilities for the DSA. Of the code administrators, Rogel has had the most impact on the code. His perspective has contributed to the most current amendment to the code, providing for review of all pyramid schemes. The amendment reads:

Pyramid Schemes
For the purpose of this Code, pyramid or endless chain schemes should be considered consumer transactions actionable under this Code. The Code Administrator shall determine whether such pyramid or endless chain schemes constitute a violation of this Code in accordance with applicable federal, state, and/or local law or regulation.

To be covered by the code, pyramid schemes were defined as consumer transactions. They are essentially commission relationships among distributors in a company where a portion of a new recruit's commissions are funneled to that individual's sponsor in the organization. Sponsors of large sales forces can generate high incomes and not make any sales themselves. In general, pyramid schemes are viewed as unfair to consumers and employees in that some individuals generate income without participating in a bona fide transaction. The rationale for classification as a consumer transaction is to enable the DSA code administrator to review the organization's commission structure and judge whether it constitutes a violation of the code.

Beyond suggesting the amendment on pyramid transactions, a number of procedural components of the code were improved, such as, the time frame for settling disputes. In the early years of the code, a consumer complaint could take up to 12 months before settlement. In the opinion of the code administrator, even if the process was working, consumers would become disgruntled in being strung along from four to nine months in various due process procedures. Even if the outcome was a finding in the customer's favor, chances were the individual would still be dissatisfied by the length of the process. Changes in code procedures now allow settlement in less than 60 days. In addition, a special fund was established in 1980 to reimburse customers for incidental expenses such as phone calls and postage incurred in building and arguing a case. The DSA contributes $5,000 yearly to the fund for distribution by the code administrator. Disbursements average from $10–$30. Over the last three years, approximately $1,200 has been used.

Outcomes of the Code: Expected and Otherwise

Over its 20-year life, the code produced both expected and unanticipated results. One obvious question is: Did the code make a difference? Before 1969, pressure from consumer groups was influencing the FTC and local jurisdictions to consider restrictions on direct selling, either in some form of licensing and registration or in a ban on direct selling in some localities. The development of the code and its supporting consumer complaint mechanism received FTC endorsement through an advisory opinion keeping strict FTC rules off the books. Moreover, in some jurisdictions (Lansing, Michigan; Prince George's County, Maryland; and Bloomington, Indiana), the code served as the basis for a model ordinance that allowed only those who subscribe to provisions like those in the code to engage in door-to-door sales. By avoiding strict restrictions on direct, in-home sales, the code, in conjunction with the self-regulation system that supports it, has made a difference. It has allowed the industry, via its association, to do something about its image problem without government intervention.

A second impact of the code was the creation of an additional step in the consumer complaint process. Traditionally, the consumer with a complaint would go to the company, then to government (consumer affairs offices) or the media for action. Now, the code administrator—not the DSA—serves as a step between the company and government to try to address the problem and gain resolution. The significance is not only in the independence of the administrator, but also in the structural arrangement that provides for resolution before resorting to government intervention and litigation. This procedure reduces costs and time spent in resolving the issue; it promotes the image of the industry in demonstrating a capacity to clean up problems caused by members.

A third impact of the code and the self-regulatory system is on applications to the DSA. Association membership is a critical seal of approval for new direct selling ventures. Before accepting a new member into the association, a DSA staff member reviews the marketing plans of the applicant. While most are approved routinely because they have acceptable plans, membership approval can be contingent on changing plans to eliminate elements of pyramid schemes. Applicants are given the opportunity to revise their marketing plans and resubmit their applications. All new members undergo a year-long screening to enable the association to observe their actual practices. According to Levering and Offen (1984), those seriously desiring membership in DSA are willing to make plan revisions as necessary and subject themselves to a year of scrutiny by the association.

Another effect of the code is the visibility it has generated with various consumer advocacy groups. Levering and Offen (1984) report ongoing relationships with the Consumer Federation of America, The National Consumer League, the National Association of Consumer Agency Administrators, and the Association for State Attorneys General, which addresses consumer fraud issues at the state level. One result of this networking is the ability to publicize the code and make these organizations aware that the consumer complaint mechanism exists. The DSA and these groups support a "cooling off" rule that allows customers three business days after a direct sale to cancel the purchase. Before this rule, customers who signed a contract and made a down payment had limited recourse if they changed their minds.

Early in the code history, the Stanley Home Products Company along with the DSA created the Zero Complaint Award. According to Offen (1976):

> This award is given by a company to its sales managers who during the course of a year have no consumer complaints lodged against them or their sales units with either the DSA, under our code of ethics, or with the company. The idea is for the field sales force to successfully handle consumer complaints on the scene, thereby keeping consumers happy and not bogging down the company or DSA with unnecessary complaint handling. At Stanley's first award ceremonies, over 25 percent of the company's 250 top managers did not have one complaint lodged against them. This represented over three million sales transactions, a truly remarkable accomplishment. The next year nearly 50 percent of the Stanley dealers qualified.

Other companies also adopted the award. The DSA recognized that competing for the award might discourage companies and their salespeople from publicizing the code. The DSA withdrew its support and the Zero Complaint Award ended in 1980.

In 1977, prior to Neil Offen taking over as president of the DSA, the organization commissioned Louis Harris to conduct a poll on the status of direct selling. It found:

- Seventy-five percent of all United States households had been contacted by people engaged in direct selling.

- Forty-nine percent of these made purchases.

- Twenty-three percent indicated that they liked this form of selling.

When those who indicated that they did not like this form of selling were asked why, their answers included the risk of opening doors to strangers, high-pressure sales techniques, and prices (Holland 1980).

The DSA used these results as an indicator that its image still needed improvement. It set a ten-year goal that, in the words of Neil Offen (1984), read: "We recognize we are guests in people's homes, and for that privilege we want to be known as the most consumer-oriented trade association in the country."

One action to move them toward this goal took place in mid-1984 when the DSA board of directors voted to repackage the code as part of the DSA Consumer Action Program (CAP). This repackaging includes programs for consumer education and awareness and complaint resolution. Motivated primarily out of (1) the need to increase awareness of the code and (2) to recognize that consumers need to understand the nature of CAP programs as complaint resolution mechanisms, the board of directors believes the repackaging will make the DSA more effective.

Beyond the effective relationships among local consumer groups, some evidence that the system is receiving attention and is producing results occurred in October 1984. The Direct Selling Association was one of eight organizations cited by the White House Office of Private Sector Initiatives for having a successful industry self-regulation program. In a keynote address, speaker James Miller III, chairman of the FTC, noted:

> The vast majority of commercial transactions work well, without need for interference of any kind, but in some cases the market fails and regulation of some kind is warranted... but this need not be government regulation if industry self-regulation is superior. And in certain instances, self-regulation can be the better choice.

Chapter 6

Defining the Self-Regulation Environment

This research project was an attempt to generate an overall appreciation of the field of self-regulation. In addition to providing answers to the basic questions, it raises new questions for future inquiry. Managers, association executives, and policymakers in the public and private sectors are beginning to realize that as a selectively used institutional arrangement, self-regulation bears consideration. It must, however, include (1) the necessary safeguards to protect the "public interest," (2) fit with current trends in regulation over standards and social performance, (3) meet the same ends in a shorter time at a lower cost, and (4) contribute to creating conditions that fundamentally change the adversarial relationship between business and government. In the emerging technical professions and the international arena, this may be vital to U.S. competitiveness.

Implications of the Study

Beyond the descriptive statistics, the major findings of the study could be summarized as follows:

Conditions. Self-regulation entails both macrolevel and microlevel decisions. Macrolevel decisions are made by government in determining whether self-regulation is an appropriate mechanism for controlling business behavior. Microlevel decisions concerning the nature and operation of the components of the system are made by the self-regulating organization (business association) and generally require government approval. By the nature of the government and membership approval process, self-regulation requires consideration of both rules formulation and implementation procedures before it is approved. Legal and economic conditions shape the possibilities for self-regulation. Organizational and political processes are the mechanisms through which the system operates.

Roles. The roles of influencing the preconditions, making rules, and enforcing rules represent an expansion of the traditional role of associations (providing information and education).

Success. Successful self-regulation is a systems concept. A successful self-regulated system requires membership approval, association presence, the existence of procedures for due process and for adapting the system as needed, and constituent contact in government (federal, state, and local levels) among the membership and among consumers.

Table 10 depicts ways of evaluating the success of a self-regulation program.

The elements of success derived from the study and noted here parallel the opinion of experts in the field. With reference to product standards, Grumbley (1982) argues that self-regulation requires some form of consensus between business and government in the following areas:

- science and technology to define the issue,

- policies and standards, and

- enforcement.

Bardach and Kagan (1982) contend that successful regulatory policy results from "new modes for organizing responsibility," and that it requires "furnishing the responsible actors as much discretion as possible in regards to means and techniques." Rogel (1984), whose experience is with codes in direct selling and advertising, notes that successful self-regulation:

- requires ongoing membership endorsement,

- assures that the system will not restrict competition, and

Table 10. Performance Indicators for Successful Self-Regulation

	Insiders (objectives)	Outsiders (expectations)
Outcomes	System approval by membership and government	Responsiveness
	Adaptation of system over time	Consumer awareness
	Association's responsibilities broadened	Removal of bad participants or companies
	Create layer of complaint resolution between firm and government	Predictability/reduction of uncertainty in transactions
	Improve image of industry	
	Save money	
Process	Ongoing cooperation with government and membership	Fairness
	No restraint of trade	
	Fairness and representation	Understandable
	Due process	
	Withstand court tests, if necessary	

- allows the use of sanctions after due process procedures are utilized.

Failures of self-regulation are explained by the absence or weakness in the critical conditions. In cases where an opportunity for self-regulation exists, an *awareness of the need* must be held by key members of the association. Differences show up in perceptions regarding the *urgency* of the problem. The opinion to "do something" may not be widely shared.

Even when self-regulation is a possible alternative, an industry may lack the *capacity* to organize a program. In the case of funeral directors, no single association represented the more than 50,000 funeral directors. For years, the FTC had encouraged them to develop a more consumer-oriented disclosure of prices and packages. Yet, no mechanism was available for the various regional and religious interests to come together to form a system. Moreover, no individual *leader* emerged to create a program.

For existing self-regulation programs that fail, the explanation is either lack of *leadership commitment* or a *structural flaw*. Top management demonstrates commitment to particular issues by involvement and participation. Support for self-regulation is no different. The commitment of resources such as staff and attention from top management is important.

The *structure* of a self-regulation program is critical. Procedures for making rules, approving amendments, and selecting committee members need to be clear and fair. The program itself needs to contain proper due process procedures and notifications.

Finally, the program needs to have teeth. This includes proper monitoring procedures, sanctions, and an enforcement mechanism. The cozy relationship among accounting firms in the peer-review system in the 1970s conveyed a lack of seriousness about their self-regulatory program. Their revitalized code of ethics in 1986 and the procedures that support it show that the industry is committed to serious self-policing.

Association Issues

Clearly, associations and professional societies play a pivotal role in developing and maintaining the self-regulatory system. The choice to get involved in the development of a self-regulation system entails

- organizational learning and evolution in terms of the association's relationship with government and its membership,

- commitment under uncertainty to generate approval and operate a system, and

- expansion of traditional association activities.

Consideration of these issues should be taken into account in the professional development of association executives.

Policy Implications

Traditionally, regulatory policy has highlighted the distinctions in the roles of government and industry decision makers. Consistent with Preston's (1986) concept of metaregulation, this study suggests that in the standards-setting area, the government's responsibility may be best served by encouraging and supporting the development of industry-based standards groups and self-regulatory associations. Part of this responsibility, however, requires the willingness of the government agency to engage in ongoing discussions and coach the self-regulatory group to insure that the system it develops complies with appropriate laws. Industry policymakers need to recognize that taking on responsibility for a self-regulation system requires an ongoing, long-term commitment to interaction with government agencies and their member organizations.

The regulatory policy arena is a major center of business-government interaction. The controversy over appropriate means that meet the desired ends of regulation will continue. Yet, with appropriate safeguards and proper planning, self-regulation may be an alternative worth acknowledging and supporting. While self-regulation is neither a panacea for addressing all forms of unwanted behavior nor a call for laissez-faire government policy, it can be of use in improving product standards and codes of conduct. It can also be of use in addressing issues of safety and performance in newly emerging industries and professional specialties. Associations (both trade groups and professional societies) clearly emerge as pivotal players in this process.

Appendix

Descriptions of Selected Self-Regulation Programs

American Association of Museums
1225 Eye St., N.W.
Washington, DC 20005
Contact: Patricia E. Williams
Organization Founded: 1906
Self-Regulation Program Developed: 1969
Membership: 650
Percent of Industry Total: 10%
Structure: Association governing body; committees and task forces develop codes, rules, and policies, then circulate to the field for comments before presentation to governing body.
Program Description: Accreditation requires the museum to organize its governing body, staff, and financial resources to focus on meeting the mission of the museum. Through self-study, which can take up to a year to complete, the museum identifies which institutional issues it needs to address to be more effective. A museum's accreditation is based on whether or not the institution is doing what it says it is doing and how well.

American Association of Occupational Health Nurses (AAOHN)
50 Lennox Pointe
Atlanta, GA 30324
Contact: Ann R. Cox
Organization Founded: 1942
Self-Regulation Program Developed: 1942
Membership: 22,000
Percent of Industry Total: 100%
Structure: Board of directors; staff and committee input, investigation, and development of ideas for board approval.
Program Description: AAOHN has a code of ethics and standards. Compliance is monitored at the state level. They work with a

certification body to promote certification, but they do not conduct certification.

American Association of School Administrators (AASA)

1801 N. Moore St.
Arlington, VA 22209
Contact: Gary Marx
Organization Founded: 1865
Self-Regulation Program Developed: N/A
Membership: 18,750
Structure: Executive committee and professional staff.
Program Description: AASA's self-regulation program provides ethical statements of standards specifically for educational administrators. As an administrator, one assumes the responsibility of providing professional leadership to the community. This responsibility, which requires the administrator to maintain standards of exemplary professional conduct, is aided and supported by AASA's self-regulation program.

American College of Foot Surgeons

1601 Dolores St.
San Francisco, CA 94110
Contact: John L. Bennett
Organization Founded: 1942
Self-Regulation Program Developed: N/A
Membership: 2,500
Percent of Industry Total: N/A
Structure: Board of directors.
Program Description: The parent organization, American Podiatric Medical Association (APMA), has a code of ethics. The College has developed a statement of professional conduct to accompany the APMA's code of ethics.

The American Humane Association, Animal Protection Division

9725 East Hampden Ave.
Denver, CO 80231
Contact: Carol Moulton
Organization Founded: 1877
Self-Regulation Program Developed: 1984
Membership: 50
Percent of Industry Total: 1.5%
Structure: Board of directors, executive staff, and advisory committee.

Program Description: The American Humane Association sponsors a Standards of Excellence program designed to increase national awareness of animal protection and to help upgrade and improve animal care and control throughout the U.S. Standards of Excellence defines standards for humane animal sheltering and control; it also identifies agencies meeting the established standards and gives substandard agencies guidelines for improvement.

American Institute of Building Design (AIBD)
1412 19th St.
Sacramento, CA 95814
Contact: Thomas Ethen
Organization Founded: 1950
Self-Regulation Program Developed: 1970s
Membership: 300
Percent of Industry Total: N/A
Structure: Board of directors and executive committee.
Program Description: AIBD created a voluntary certification program for professional building designers. Certification as a professional building designer by the Institute attests the individual as fully qualified to perform all requisite technical aspects of his or her profession and as competent to execute his or her duties. Successful completion of the Institute exam permits the certified professional building designer to use a seal or stamp bearing his or her name and Institute certification number for use on plans and documents. AIBD also censures improprieties and violations of state building codes.

American Institute of Professional Geologists
7828 Vance Dr., Suite 103
Arvada, CO 80003
Contact: Carol A. Beckett
Organization Founded: 1963
Self-Regulation Program Developed: 1963
Membership: 45,000
Percent of Industry Total: N/A
Structure: Executive committee.
Program Description: The Institute's purpose is to strengthen the geological sciences as a profession with all reasonable actions to establish professional qualifications, to certify those qualifications to the public, and to evaluate continuously the ethical conduct of its members. Further, the Institute establishes ethical

standards to protect the public and the geological sciences from nonprofessional practices.

American National Standards Institute (ANSI)

1430 Broadway
New York, NY 10018
Contact: William H. Rockwell
Organization Founded: 1918
Self-Regulation Program Developed: 1918
Membership: 20,000
Percent of Industry Total: 90%
Structure: Board of directors and executive standards council.
Program Description: ANSI, through its executive standards council and coordinating boards and committees, provides a structure and climate where voluntary standards activities are coordinated. Specifically, ANSI (1) coordinates voluntary standards activities in the U.S., (2) serves as the U.S. member of the International Organization for Standardization and the International Electrotechnical Commission, (3) provides forums for government-industry cooperation, and (4) is the clearinghouse and central source for information on national and international standards.

American Nuclear Society (ANS)

555 N. Kensington Ave.
LaGrange Park, IL 60525
Contact: Octave J. Du Temple
Organization Founded: 1954
Self-Regulation Program Developed: 1958
Membership: 10,000 individuals; 230 organizations
Percent of Industry Total: 90%
Structure: Volunteers are the key individuals responsible for program development.
Program Description: The American Nuclear Society's self-regulation programs are coordinated with the Accreditation Board for Engineering and Technology (ABET) and with American Nuclear Standards Institute (ANSI). Through ABET, the ANS sets the education standards for training nuclear engineers. Under ANSI, the ANS develops standards for design and construction of nuclear facilities and associated equipment; it also develops standards for safe training and operation of these facilities.

The American Society of CLU and CHFC

270 Bryn Mawr Ave.
Bryn Mawr, PA 19010

Contact: Burke Christensen
Organization Founded: 1928
Self-Regulation Program Developed: N/A
Membership: 30,000
Percent of Industry Total: 13%
Structure: Board of directors and ethical guidance committee.
Program Description: Enforcement of a professional code of ethics is conducted primarily by the local chapter's ethical guidance committee, with review by the national ethical guidance committee.

American Society of Civil Engineers
345 E. 47th St.
New York, NY 10017
Contact: A. Buzzell
Organization Founded: 1858
Self-Regulation Program Developed: 1914
Membership: 103,000
Percent of Industry Total: 50%
Structure: Board of directors, committee on professional voluntary conduct, and staff.
Program Description: Members are required to pledge compliance with society's code of ethics with membership application. The committee on professional conduct investigates all ethics violation complaints, including news accounts. Results may be published and reported to the State Board of Registration, as appropriate.

American Society of Cytology
1015 Chestnut St., Suite 1518
Philadelphia, PA 19107
Contact: Bernard Naylor
Organization Founded: 1951
Self-Regulation Program Developed: 1970
Membership: 47 cytotechnologists; 46 cytopathology labs
Percent of Industry Total: 100%; 10%
Structure: Cytotechnology program committee, committee on allied health education and accreditation, and volunteers.
Program Description: The American Society of Cytology conducts two accrediting educational programs: (1) for cytotechnologists, to ensure they reach a satisfactory level of competence for future laboratory work, and (2) for the laboratories practicing cytopathology, to ensure that satisfactory standards of practice and competence are maintained.

Association of College, University and Community Arts Administrators (ACUCAA)
1112 16th St., N.W., Suite 620
Washington, DC 20036
Contact: Evan Kavanaugh
Organization Founded: 1956
Self-Regulation Program Developed: 1970 and 1978
Membership: 1,500
Percent of Industry Total: 20%
Structure: Board of directors.
Program Description: ACUCAA has recently abandoned its informal enforcement program in favor of an education program to teach members exactly what constitutes ethical behavior. In addition, a mediation service is planned to provide nonjudicial dispute resolution between active affiliate members (such as theaters, artist managements).

Board of Certified Safety Professionals (BCSP)
208 Burwash Ave.
Savoy, IL 61874
Contact: Michael K. Orn
Organization Founded: 1969
Self-Regulation Program Developed: 1969
Membership: 7,000
Percent of Industry Total: 25%
Structure: Board of directors, with input from those certified in the field and committee study.
Program Description: The BCSP has established academic and experience requirements necessary for certification as a Certified Safety Professional, Associate Safety Professional, or other designations established by the board of directors. BCSP conducts investigations and examinations verifying the qualifications of candidates for certification. A Certified Safety Professional uses knowledge of engineering and the various human and physical sciences in the development of procedures, processes, specifications, and systems to achieve control and reduction of hazards and exposures detrimental to life, health, and property.

Canadian Association of Custom Brokers (CACB)
121 York St.
Ottawa, Ontario, Canada
Contact: Janice Payn

Organization Founded: 1920
Self-Regulation Program Developed: N/A
Membership: 292
Percent of Industry Total: 80%
Structure: Board of directors, national committee structure, two-thirds membership approval necessary for amendment of bylaws.
Program Description: Members upon entry into and during membership in the CACB are expected to abide by the code of ethics presented in the CACB bylaws. Complaints are reviewed in accordance with due process by a discipline committee composed of no less than five CACB members. Committee members are appointed by the chairman.

Canadian Nurses Association (CNA)
50 The Driveway
Ottawa, Ontario, Canada
Contact: Ginette Rodger
Organization Founded: 1908
Self-Regulation Program Developed: N/A
Membership: 200,000
Percent of Industry Total: 99%
Structure: Board; a board committee establishes policies and staff for implementation; the committee of the board also helps develop rules.
Program Description: CNA is a federation of 11 provincial/territorial members; most of them are registration bodies. The regulation program includes: (1) national/provincial standards of nursing practice administration and education, (2) national/provincial code of ethics, (3) national registration teams for candidates entering the profession, and (4) national certification for nurses working in a specialty area.

College Art Association of America (CAA)
275 Seventh Ave.
New York, NY 10001
Contact: Ruth Weisberg
Organization Founded: 1911
Self-Regulation Program Developed: 1973
Membership: N/A
Percent of Industry Total: N/A
Structure: Board committee; support and guidance from a long-range planning committee.
Program Description: CAA's code of ethics for art historians

encompasses practices governing the teaching profession, practices governing right of access to information and responsibilities of scholars, responsibilities of scholars to discourage illegal traffic in works of art, and guidelines for the professional practices of art history. CAA's code of ethics for artists encompasses instruction on safe use of materials and equipment, recommended use of copyright notice, and guidelines for the professional practice of studio art.

Computer Dealers & Lessors Association (CDLA)

1212 Potomac St., N.W.
Washington, DC 20007
Contact: Dianne L. Sims
Organization Founded: 1967
Self-Regulation Program Developed: 1967
Membership: N/A
Percent of Industry Total: 100%
Structure: Board of directors and the association's industry practices committee.
Program Description: CDLA works closely with those in the business of leasing computers and trading in used computers. This organization's primary job is to aid its members in doing business in a "more efficient and profitable manner." They accomplish their primary objective by writing newsletters, holding industry meetings and special seminars, communicating with members and with the federal government on taxation issues, giving their opinion to the trade and national press, enforcing the industry practices code, holding meetings for the exchange of ideas and addressing pocketbook issues that will affect the day-to-day business.

Cosmetic Toiletry & Fragrance Association (CTFA)

1110 Vermont Ave., N.W.
Washington, DC 20005
Contact: Mark A. Pollakk
Organization Founded: 1984
Self-Regulation Program Developed: N/A
Membership: 1,000
Percent of Industry Total: 50%
Structure: CTFA board members and FDA chief council; also a steering committee.
Program Description: The Cosmetic Ingredient Review was established in 1976 by CTFA, to review and document the safety

of ingredients used in cosmetic products. CTFA, an independent, nonprofit organization, was established to evaluate data concerning ingredient safety under formalized procedures that closely parallel those of the FDA's advisory panels for the over-the-counter drug review program.

Council of Community Blood Centers (CCBC)

725 15th St., N.W., Suite 700
Washington, DC 20005
Contact: J. MacPherson
Organization Founded: 1962
Self-Regulation Program Developed: 1982
Membership: 31
Percent of Industry Total: 25%
Structure: Board of trustees (comprising one voting representative from each institutional member).
Program Description: CCBC establishes its self-regulation program to represent the common concerns of community blood programs and serve as a forum for addressing the needs of those involved in blood center operation. CCBC is dedicated to serving the public by promoting excellence in blood services. It is the common endeavor of CCBC to improve the quality and efficiency of blood services to the community and the nation. The scope of CCBC's activities and services range from practical details of day-to-day blood center operations to addressing major national policy issues. CCBC has a multifaceted program that addresses the significant areas of operation of a community blood center, as well as the medical, scientific, technical, and administrative areas.

The Council for Exceptional Children

1920 Association Dr.
Reston, VA 22091
Contact: Kayte M. Fearn
Organization Founded: 1922
Self-Regulation Program Developed: 1983
Membership: N/A
Percent of Industry Total: N/A
Structure: Board of governors, delegate assembly, and professional standards committee.
Program Description: The Council for Exceptional Children, as a constituent member of the National Council for Accreditation of Teacher Education, develops and implements standards for the

special education community in ethics, practice, and personal preparation. In addition, they are developing policies for special education certification.

Council on Postsecondary Accreditation (COPA)

One Dupont Circle, N.W., Suite 305
Washington, DC 20036
Contact: Donald B. Kaveny
Organization Founded: 1975
Self-Regulation Program Developed: 1975
Membership: 60
Percent of Industry Total: N/A
Structure: Board of directors, committees, and assembly.
Program Description: The purpose of the Council is to monitor the accreditation community and the new accrediting bodies. The education accreditation community comes together under the auspices of COPA to regulate itself and maintain the integrity of the education community.

Evangelical Council for Financial Accountability (ECFA)

P.O. Box 17465
Washington, DC 20041
Contact: Arthur C. Borden
Organization Founded: 1979
Self-Regulation Program Developed: 1979
Membership: 500
Percent of Industry Total: N/A
Structure: Board of directors, standards committee, and staff.
Program Description: ECFA was established to address the concerns among evangelical ministries regarding the handling of finances. By setting standards for the handling of finances, ECFA's mission is to increase the public's confidence in the business affairs of evangelical organizations. Membership into ECFA is limited to nonprofit evangelical Christian organizations. The ECFA mission statement outlines the organization's goal as increasing public confidence in the business affairs of evangelical organizations by establishing standards, helping organizations meet the standards, certifying compliance, and communicating with the public.

Eye Bank Association of America, Inc.

1725 Eye St., N.W.
Washington, DC 20006
Contact: Tom Moore

Organization Founded: 1961
Self-Regulation Program Developed: 1981
Membership: 92
Percent of Industry Total: 95%
Structure: A medical standards policy committee sets policies and procedures.
Program Description: A certification program for eye banks is conducted based upon medical standards accepted in the industry. This certification process requires a peer review site visit every three years. Technicians are certified through an examination administered by the association. Recertification of the technicians occurs every three years through professional certification credits.

Florists' Transworld Delivery Association
29200 Northwest Hwy.
Southfield, MI 48034
Contact: Jack LaRue
Organization Founded: 1910
Self-Regulation Program Developed: 1960
Membership: 24,000
Percent of Industry Total: 65%
Structure: Board of directors and committees.
Program Description: The association's self-regulation program consists of a body of membership rules, which a member agrees to abide by once membership is granted. Before membership is granted, applicants must meet a body of requirements for membership. The membership division evaluates applicants and monitors compliance of members with membership rules through various tests and inspections. The membership division also works with a membership committee on discipline of members.

Glass Packing Institute
1801 K St., N.W.
Washington, DC 20006
Contact: H. Bologh
Organization Founded: 1945
Self-Regulation Program Developed: 1945
Membership: 25
Percent of Industry Total: 100%
Structure: Board of directors; new standards/revisions reviewed and decided upon by subcommittees.
Program Description: Product standards are established and main-

tained for items manufactured by two or more manufacturers for two or more customers. The process is available to the entire industry. Manufacturer representatives gather as a collective body on a volunteer basis to develop and review standards. Manufacturers and customers are free to use or not use the standards available.

Health Sciences Communications Association

6105 Lindell Blvd.
St. Louis, MO 63112
Contact: L. Elsesser
Organization Founded: 1959
Self-Regulation Program Developed: 1987
Membership: 600
Percent of Industry Total: N/A
Structure: Board of directors and volunteers.
Program Description: Through their code of ethics, the Health Sciences Communications Association established voluntary guidelines for the ethical treatment and rendering of service to clients, patients, and colleagues.

Holstein-Friesian Association of America

One Holstein Place
Brattleboro, VT 05301
Contact: Zane Akins
Organization Founded: 1885
Self-Regulation Program Developed: 1930
Membership: 200,000
Percent of Industry Total: 100%
Structure: Board of directors.
Program Description: This organization has a regulatory function in maintaining orderliness and discipline among all who participate in the registered holstein industry. Credibility and the genealogical and performance records are critical. While the bylaws give direction to this regulatory function, it provides for a separate document entitled "Rules to Preserve Integrity and for Hearings and Appeals." This is supplemented by several other policy documents such as the Merchandising Policy, giving credence and orderliness in merchandising registered holsteins; the Show Ring Policy, setting standards for exhibition of cattle in the show ring; and Rules for Production Testing to maintain credibility of performance.

International Concatenated Order of Hoo-Hoo

P.O. Box 118
Gurdon, AR 71743
Contact: Billy Tarpley
Organization Founded: 1892
Self-Regulation Program Developed: 1921
Membership: 7,000
Percent of Industry Total: N/A
Structure: N/A
Program Description: Hoo-Hoo International's code of ethics lists nine aims to further the credibility of persons engaged in the lumber industry. Cited below are aims two and eight, respectively, to exemplify the essence of their overall goals:
- to promote human advancement and higher standards of civic, social, and economic relations by developing in business the spirit of the Golden Rule, which we accept as the basic principle of peace and prosperity for the world;
- to keep in view the world bonds of human interest and trade, seeking to promote friendly understanding among all nations and races.

Hotel and Motel Brokers of America

10920 Ambassador Dr., Suite 520
Kansas City, MO 64153
Contact: Bob Krolicak
Organization Founded: N/A
Self-Regulation Program Developed: 1979
Membership: 125 individuals; 30 firms
Percent of Industry Total: N/A
Structure: Board of directors and ethics committee.
Program Description: The self-regulation program consists of a code of ethics with a review committee that makes recommendations to the board of directors. Dispute resolution is handled by the American Arbitration Association after preliminary review by a complaint committee.

IDEA Foundation

6190 Cornerstone Ct., Suite 202
San Diego, CA 92122
Contact: Sheryl Marks
Organization Founded: 1985
Self-Regulation Program Developed: 1986
Membership: 9,000

Percent of Industry Total: 9%

Structure: Executive director and over 75 key professionals in the industry.

Program Description: The IDEA Foundation is a nonprofit organization committed to promoting safe and effective exercise to the consumer while adding quality and credibility to the exercise profession. The foundation accomplishes its mission through consumer education, research, certification of exercise instructors, and the promotion of quality education programs.

Independent Lubricant Manufacturers Association (ILMA)

1055 Thomas Jefferson St., N.W.
Washington, DC 20007

Contact: Nancy DeMarco
Organization Founded: 1948
Self-Regulation Program Developed: 1984
Membership: 160 firms
Percent of Industry Total: 75%
Structure: Board of directors, executive director, and ethics committee.

Program Description: Via ILMA's code of ethics, rules have been established that provide mandatory and specific standards for professional conduct in the lubricating industry. The rules of ethics are enforceable by the association under procedures provided in their code of ethics.

In-Plant Management Association (IPMA)

1205 West College Ave.
Liberty, MO 64068

Contact: Larry E. Aaron
Organization Founded: 1964
Self-Regulation Program Developed: 1976
Membership: 375
Percent of Industry Total: 1%
Structure: Board of directors and certification committee.

Program Description: IPMA's Certified Graphics Communication Management (CGCM) program established a professional proficiency standard for the in-plant graphic arts and printing management profession. CGCM, a voluntary program, awards certification to participants who demonstrate management experience and professionalism. In addition, participants must achieve successful completion of a comprehensive examination prepared by the IPMA international certification committee. Procedures are also in place for recertification every five years.

Institute for Certification of Computer Professionals (ICCP)

2200 E. Devon Ave., Suite 268
Des Plaines, IL 60018
Contact: George R. Eggert
Organization Founded: 1973
Self-Regulation Program Developed: 1973
Membership: 43,000
Percent of Industry Total: N/A
Structure: Board of directors.
Program Description: ICCP promotes high standards of excellence for members in the computer profession through its certification program. ICCP's established code of ethics and code of conduct and good practice serve to strengthen the professional status of certified computer professionals.

Institute of Internal Auditors

249 Maitland Ave.
Altamonte Springs, FL 32071
Contact: Thomas E. Powell
Organization Founded: 1941
Self-Regulation Program Developed: 1968
Membership: 32,000
Percent of Industry Total: N/A
Structure: Board of directors, professional standards committee.
Program Description: The professional standards committee is responsible for receiving, interpreting, and investigating all complaints on behalf of the board of directors, and appropriately recommending to the board of directors actions be taken.

Institute of Management Consultants, Inc.

19 West 44th St., Suite 810
New York, NY 10036
Contact: John F. Hartshorne
Organization Founded: 1968
Self-Regulation Program Developed: 1968
Membership: 1,500
Percent of Industry Total: 3%
Structure: Board of directors, standing committees, and volunteers.
Program Description: The mission of the Institute is to improve the practice of management consulting and the public's perception of it. To this end, the Institute:

- promotes high standards in the conduct of professional management consulting,
- communicates those standards to the public,
- accredits as Certified Management Consultants members of demonstrated competence who have agreed to uphold the Institute's standards as a continuing condition of individual certification, and
- accepts as associate members others in the practice of management consulting who are working toward certification and who have agreed to uphold the Institute's standards as a continuing condition of membership.

Accredited members of the Institute are authorized to use the title "Certified Management Consultant" (CMC).

International Association of Assessing Officers

1313 E. 60th St.
Chicago, IL 60637
Contact: Richard R. Almy
Organization Founded: 1934
Self-Regulation Program Developed: 53
Membership: 7,900
Percent of Industry Total: N/A
Structure: Executive board, committees, staff, and volunteers.
Program Description: The International Association of Assessing Officers seeks to improve standards of assessment practice by developing and enforcing its code of ethics and standards of professional conduct, which incorporates the Uniform Standards of Professional Appraisal Practice; by conferring designations on individuals who have demonstrated mastery of appraisal principles, mass appraisal techniques, and administration; by developing voluntary "assessment standards" that comprehensively define a model of assessment administration; and by carrying out related activities.

International Association of Hospitality Accountants

P.O. Box 27649
Austin, TX 78755
Contact: Barbara Byrd-Lawler
Organization Founded: 1955
Self-Regulation Program Developed: 1980
Membership: 289
Percent of Industry Total: 25%

Structure: Executive committee, staff, and volunteers.

Program Description: The purpose of the International Association of Hospitality Accountants is to educate, develop, and provide support for the profession of accounting, financial management, and information processing within the hospitality industry. Through this certification program, IAHA grants use of the title Certified Hospitality Account Executive (CHAE) to members successfully completing a written certification exam. CHAEs have the following objectives:

- to cultivate professional cooperation among the members of IAHA,
- to encourage the education and advancement of IAHA members,
- to provide professional recognition to IAHA members who have acquired the basic educational proficiencies and practical experiences that signify successful career progression.

International Association of Refrigerated Warehouses

7315 Wisconsin Ave., Suite 1200 N
Bethesda, MD 20814

Contact: J. William Hudson
Organization Founded: 1891
Self-Regulation Program Developed: 1970
Membership: 5,000
Percent of Industry Total: 90%
Structure: Upper-level management and a round table committee that receives input from 17 associations.
Program Description: An industry code of recommended practices for the proper handling of frozen foods was established through the frozen food round table.

International Association of Wiping Cloth Manufacturers

7410 Woodmont Ave., Suite 1212
Bethesda, MD 20814

Contact: Bernard D. Brill
Organization Founded: 1932
Self-Regulation Program Developed: 1976
Membership: Approximately 150
Percent of Industry Total: 90%
Structure: N/A
Program Description: In the wiping materials business, there are many different fabrics, colors, and quantities produced.

Standards help classify these variables as well as discrepancies about weight.

International Bottled Water Association (IBWA)

113 N. Henry St.
Alexandria, VA 22314
Contact: William Deal
Organization Founded: 1958
Self-Regulation Program Developed: 1976
Membership: 210
Percent of Industry Total: 85%
Structure: Board of directors.
Program Description: The following objectives, extracted from those listed in the IBWA's bylaws, summarize the association's purpose:
- to serve as the authoritative source of information...about all types of bottled waters and their respective advantages;
- to diligently pursue, through public, legislative, and regulatory bodies, those legislative and regulatory actions which will affect all types of bottled water and to work closely with all government agencies whose regulations affect the bottled water industry and the standards of quality and/or purity of bottled water;
- to establish a continuing education program and technical assistance to industry members;
- to help the industry attain and maintain high standards of quality and sanitation through annual inspections of its member companies to the highest possible level.

International Council of Nurses (ICN)

3, Place Jean-Marteau
CH-1201 Geneva, Switzerland
Contact: Constance A. Holleran
Organization Founded: 1899
Self-Regulation Program Developed: 1953
Membership: N/A
Percent of Industry Total: N/A
Structure: Board of directors, staff, and voting body.
Program Description: ICN encourages national nurses associations to take a more active role in establishing the appropriate system for regulating the practice of nursing, while at the same time making it possible for the knowledge and skills of nurses to be more effectively utilized and recognized. ICN's Code for Nurses provides necessary ethical guidance required by nurses in a

rapidly changing world with constant social, technological, genetic, and pharmacological advances.

International Credit Association
243 North Lindbergh
St. Louis, MO 43141
Contact: William J. Henderson
Organization Founded: 1912
Self-Regulation Program Developed: 1961
Membership: 3,232
Percent of Industry Total: N/A
Structure: Board of directors and executive committee.
Program Description: International's program is designed specifically for the credit professional. Their established certification program is available to persons currently employed in the credit industry. Certification is offered on three progressive levels: (1) Credit Associate, (2) Associate Credit Executive, and (3) Certified Consumer Credit Executive, Certified Credit Bureau Executive, Collection Agency Executive, Financial Counseling Executive. Final decisions concerning qualifications for certification rest with the board of trustees.

National Association of Housing and Redevelopment Officials
1320 18th St., N.W.
Washington, DC 20036
Contact: Letitia Combs
Organization Founded: 1934
Self-Regulation Program Developed: 1978
Membership: 10,000
Percent of Industry Total: N/A
Structure: Board of credentialing trustees, experienced professional housing managers.
Program Description: The board of credentialing trustees oversees certification; Housing and Urban Development is responsible for enforcement action. Public Housing Management assesses the individual's ability to meet required standards of professional performance as managers of public housing.

National Association of Life Underwriters (NALU)
1922 F. St., N.W.
Washington, DC 20006
Contact: Jack E. Bobo

Organization Founded: 1890
Self-Regulation Program Developed: 1890
Membership: 140,000
Percent of Industry Total: 70%
Structure: Board of directors, national council, and volunteers.
Program Description: NALU is a federation offering guidance, legal assistance, and standardization. The presence of the program is an effective deterrent to misconduct; denial of membership causes loss of important benefits (prestige, awards). All control of individuals rests with local associations; only locals can expel a member.

National Board of Pediatric Nurse Practitioners and Associates

416 Hungerford Dr., Suite 411
Rockville, MD 20850
Contact: Nancy D. Hazard
Organization Founded: 1975
Self-Regulation Program Developed: 1975
Membership: 3,430
Percent of Industry Total: 50%
Structure: Executive committee, staff, and volunteers.
Program Description: The National Board of Pediatric Nurse Practitioners and Associates is a nonprofit organization which promotes quality pediatric health care through the certification and certification maintenance programs for nurses functioning in either the general pediatric nursing or pediatric nurse practitioner role.

National Contract Management Association (NCMA)

1912 Woodford Rd.
Vienna, VA 22180
Contact: James W. Goggins
Organization Founded: 1959
Self-Regulation Program Developed: 1975
Membership: 23,500
Percent of Industry Total: 100%
Structure: Board of directors, executive committee, and staff.
Program Description: NCMA provides and maintains standards of proficiency and ethics through a national certification program at two levels: Certified Professional Contracts Manager and Certified Associated Contracts Manager. Recertification is required every five years.

National Commission on Certification of Physician Assistants (NCCPA)
2845 Henderson Hill Rd.
Atlanta, GA 30341
Contact: David L. Glazer
Organization Founded: 1973
Self-Regulation Program Developed: N/A
Membership: N/A
Percent of Industry Total: N/A
Structure: Board of directors, executive committee, and staff.
Program Description: NCCPA is a certifying board that is independent of the professional society; it attests, through examination, to the competence of physician assistants on a voluntary basis. Their certificate is a prerequisite to practice in over 40 states by statute or regulation.

National Dairy Herd Improvement Association, Inc. (NDHIA)
3021 East Dublin-Granville Rd.
Columbus, OH 43231
Contact: Frank N. Dickson
Organization Founded: 1965
Self-Regulation Program Developed: 1980
Membership: 43
Percent of Industry Total: 98%
Structure: Board of directors.
Program Description: The NDHIA, Inc., self-regulation program is designed to (1) ensure accurate equipment, approve procedures, and timely performance in providing service to dairy farmer members, and (2) assure that information generated by the program has a high degree of accuracy and reliability for all uses.

National Frame Builders Association
712 Broadway, Suite 605
Kansas City, MO 64105
Contact: James T. Knight
Organization Founded: 1971
Self-Regulation Program Developed: 1974
Membership: N/A
Percent of Industry Total: 100%
Structure: Board of directors.
Program Description: The National Frame Builders Association has

promulgated "Standards of Professional Conduct" that all members are required to adhere to by virtue of so indicating on their application of membership.

National Hearing Aid Society

20361 Middlebelt
Livonia, MI 48152
Contact: Anthony DiRocco
Organization Founded: 1951
Self-Regulation Program Developed: 1951
Membership: 2,500
Percent of Industry Total: 25%
Structure: Board of governors, officers, and volunteers.
Program Description: The National Hearing Aid Society's aim is to promote the welfare, insofar as hearing is concerned, of the hearing impaired. The Society works to establish educational and technical standards in aural rehabilitation and provide a unified voice for those engaged in the practice of testing human hearing, as well as those for selecting, fitting, counseling, and dispensing hearing instruments. The Society grants the title "Certified Hearing Aid Audiologist" to hearing aid dealers/consultants who meet exacting standards in education, experience, competence, and character.

National Intramural-Recreational Sports Association

Gill Coliseum
221 Oregon State University
Corvalles, OR 97331
Contact: William Holsberry
Organization Founded: 1950
*Self-Regulation Program Developed:*1979
Membership: 1,000
Percent of Industry Total: 20%
Structure: National committee.
Program Description: The purposes of the Recreational Specialist Certification Program are to (1) maintain a high quality of professional competence of recreational sports specialists; (2) provide a means of identifying individuals who possess the necessary knowledge and expertise required of specialists in the field; (3) promote the educational standards set forth for the recreational sports specialists; and (4) encourage professional growth and development of recreational sports personnel.

Professional Photographers of America, Inc.

1090 Executive Way
Des Plaines, IL 60018
Contact: Robert E. Becker
Organization Founded: 1880
Self-Regulation Program Developed: 1980
Membership: 1,000
Percent of Industry Total: 1%
Structure: Board of directors; committees and trained panels.
Program Description: Program is designed to certify minimum standards capability for professional photographers doing photography satisfactorily for a consumer.

Society of Fire Protection Engineers

60 Batterymarch Street
Boston, MA 02110
Contact: D. Peter Lund
Organization Founded: 1950
Self-Regulation Program Developed: 1960s
Membership: 3,250
Percent of Industry Total: N/A
Structure: Board of directors, ethics committee.
Program Description: The Society has established a code of professional ethics with 13 canons in the areas of knowledge and skill, honesty and impartiality, and competence and prestige.

Society of Logistics Engineers

125 West Park Loop, Suite 201
Huntsville, AL 35806
Contact: Robert R. Leonard
Self-Regulation Program Developed: 1966
Membership: 10,000
Percent of Industry Total: 5%
Structure: Board of directors, executive board, and ethics committee.
Program Description: A five-member ethics committee reviews individuals' actions/activities that appear to be in violation of the Society's code of ethics. Disciplinary action ranges from verbal reprimand to membership termination. Members have the right to appeal to the Society's board of directors any decision made by a nine-member executive board.

Bibliography

Ackerman, R.W. 1973. How companies respond to social demands. *Harvard Business Review*, pp. 88–98.

Ackoff, R. 1974. *Redesigning the future.* New York: John Wiley.

Aldrich, H. 1976. Resource dependence and interorganization relations. *Administration and Society*, 7, pp. 419–54.

Aldrich, H., & Whetten, D. 1981. Organization sets, action sets, and networks: Making the most of simplicity. In P. Nystrom & W. Starbuck, eds. *Handbook of organizational design*, London: Oxford University Press.

Allison, G.T. 1971. *Essence of decision: Explaining the Cuban Missile Crisis.* Boston: Little, Brown.

American Collectors Association. 1984, June. *Rules and regulations: Code of ethics and operations.* Adopted July 1, 1971; amended January 1975, June 1976, and June 1984.

American Express. 1985. *Project Hometown America: Fact sheet.* Unpublished corporate document.

American Express. 1986. *Project Hometown America: 205 promising solutions.* Unpublished corporate document.

Andrews, K. 1980. *The concept of corporate strategy.* Homewood, IL: Richard D. Irwin.

Ansoff, I. 1984. *Implanting corporate strategy.* Englewood Cliffs, NJ: Prentice-Hall.

Arnold, G. 1984, June 23. Between PG and R. *The Washington Post*, p. C1–7.

Arrington, C., Jr., & Sawaya, R. 1984. Managing public affairs: Issues management in an uncertain environment. *California Management Review*, 26, pp. 148–60.

Arrow, J.K. 1974. *The limits of organization.* New York: W.W. Norton.

Ashby, R. 1960. *Design for a brain.* London: Chapman and Hall.

Austrom, D., & Lad, L. 1986. Problem-solving networks: Towards a synthesis of innovative approaches to social issues management. In J. Pearce II & R. Robinson, eds. *Academy of Management Best Papers Proceedings 1986*, pp. 311–15. Columbia: Academy of Management, University of South Carolina.

Averich, H., & Johnson, L.L. 1962. Behavior of the firm under regulatory constraint. *American Economic Review*, 52, pp. 1053–69.

Bain, J. 1968. *Industrial organization*. New York: John Wiley.

Bardach, E., & Kagan, R.A., eds. 1982. *Social regulation: Strategies for reform*. San Francisco, CA: ICS Press.

Barnard, C. 1938. *The functions of the executive*. Cambridge, MA: Harvard University Press.

Bauer, R.A. 1978. The corporate response process. In L. Preston, ed. *Research in corporate social performance and policy*, vol. 1. Greenwich, CT: JAI Press.

Bauer, R.A., & Gergen, K.J., eds. 1968. *The study of policy formation*. New York: Free Press.

Bauer, R.A., Pool, I.S., & Dexter, L.A. 1964. *American business and public policy: The politics of foreign trade*. New York: Atherton Press.

Beer, S. 1969. *Cybernetic systems*. London: Basic Books.

Bell, H. 1974. Self-regulation by the advertising industry. In S.P. Sethi, ed. *The unstable ground: Corporate social policy in a dynamic society*, pp. 472–82. Los Angeles: Melville Publishing.

Benson, J. 1975. The interorganizational network as a political economy. *Administrative Science Quarterly*, 20, pp. 229–49.

Berger, B., & Callahan, S. 1981. *Child care and mediating structures*. Washington, DC: American Enterprise Institute.

Berger, P.L., & Neuhaus, R.J. 1977. *To empower people: The role of mediating structures in public policy*. Washington, DC: American Enterprise Institute.

Bernstein, M.H., 1955. *Regulating business by independent commission*. Princeton, NJ: Princeton University Press.

Boddewyn, J. 1981. The global spread of advertising regulation. *MSU Business Topics*, 29, pp. 5–13.

Braemer, R.J. 1968. Disciplinary procedures for trade and professional associations. *BusinessLawyer*, 23 (4): 959–70.

Braybrooke, D., & Lindblom, C.E. 1970. *A strategy of decision*. New York: Free Press.

Breitenberg, A., & Atkins, R.G. 1981, September. *Consumer representation in standards development: Literature review and issue identification*. U.S. Department of Commerce/National Bureau of Standards, NBSIR 81-2336.

Brenner, P., Borosage, R., & Weidner, B. 1974. *Exploring contradictions: Political economy in the corporate state*. New York: McKay and Co.

Breyer, S. 1982. *Regulation and its reform*. Cambridge, MA: Harvard University Press.

Brock, G. 1975. Competition, standards, and self-regulation in the computer industry. In R.E. Caves & M.J. Roberts, eds. *Regulating the product: Quality and variety*, pp. 75–96. Cambridge, MA: Ballinger Publishing Co.

Butler, R. 1983. A transactional approach to organizing efficiency: Perspectives from markets, hierarchies, and collectives. *Administration and Society*, 15 (3): 323–62.

Caves, R.E. 1977. *American industry: Structure, conduct, and performance*. 4th ed. Englewood Cliffs, NJ: Prentice-Hall.

Caves, R.E., & Roberts, M.J., eds. 1975. *Regulating the product: Quality and variety*. Cambridge, MA: Ballinger Publishing Co.

Chandler, A.D. 1962. *Strategy and structure*. New York: Doubleday.

Chase, W. 1982. Issues management conference—A special report. *Corporate public issues and their management*, 7, pp. 1–2.

Chatov, R. 1975. *Corporate financial reporting: Public or private control*. New York: Free Press.

Chatov, R. 1978. Government regulation: Process and substantive impacts. In L. Preston, ed. *Research in corporate social performance and policy*, vol. 1. Greenwich, CT: JAI Press.

Churchman, C.W. 1974. *The design of inquiring systems: basic concepts of systems and organizations*. New York: Basic Books.

Clark, M., & Witherspoon, D. 1984, December 31. Still too many caesareans? *Newsweek*, p. 70.

Clinard, M.B., & Yeager, P.C. 1980. *Corporate crime*. New York: Free Press.

Coates, J., Coates, V., Jarratt, J., & Heinz, L. 1986. *Issues management: How you can plan, organize, and manage for the future*. Mt. Airy, MD: Lomond Publications.

Commons, J. 1959. *Institutional economics*. Madison, WI: University of Wisconsin Press.

Council of Better Business Bureaus, Inc./National Advertising Division. 1985, January 15. *NAD Case Report*, 14(12), pp. 43–45.

Crock, S. 1981, April 30. Product safety agency fights cuts in budget and power as Congress mulls role of regulators. *Wall Street Journal*, p. 56.

Cummings, T. 1984. Transorganizational development. In B. Staw & T. Cummings, eds. *Research in organizational behavior*, 5. Greenwich, CT: JAI Press.

Cyert, R.M., & March, J.G. 1963. *A behavioral theory of the firm*. Englewood Cliffs, NJ: Prentice-Hall.

Dahl, R.A. 1959. Business and politics: A critical appraisal of political science. In R.A. Dahl, M. Haire, and P.F. Lazarsfeld, eds. *Social science research on business: Product and potential.* New York: Columbia University Press.

Deutsch, M. 1949. An experimental study of the effects of cooperation and competition upon group processes. *Human Relations,* 2, pp. 199–231.

Dinkins, C.E. 1984, October 3. Address before White House Conference on Association Self-Regulation, Washington, DC.

Dixon, G., Jr. 1978. *Standards development in the private sector: Thoughts on interest representation and procedural fairness.* Boston: National Fire Protection Association.

Dixon, W. 1968. Self-regulation: panacea or pitfall. *University of Richmond Law Review,* 29 pp. 35–36.

Drucker, P. 1984. Doing good to do well: The new opportunities for business enterprise. In H. Brooks, L. Liebman, & C. Schelling, eds. *Public-private partnership: New opportunities for meeting social needs.* Cambridge, MA: Ballinger Publishing Co.

Dunlop, J., ed. 1980. *Business and public policy.* Cambridge, MA: Harvard University Press.

Emery, F., & Trist, E. 1973. *Towards a social ecology.* New York: Plenum.

Epstein, E. 1980. Business political activity: Research approaches and analytical issues. In L. Preston, ed. *Research in corporate social performance and policy,* vol. 2. Greenwich: CT: JAI Press.

Epstein, E. 1969. *The corporation in American politics.* Englewood Cliffs, NJ: Prentice-Hall, pp. 192–221.

Epstein, E. 1979, May. Societal, managerial, and legal perspectives on corporate social responsibility—product and process. *The Hastings Law Journal,* 30, pp. 1287–1320.

Evan, W.M. 1972. An organization-set model of interorganizational relations. In M.F. Tuite, et. al. *Interorganizational decision-making.* Concord: Aldine-Atherton Publishing Co.

Evan, W.M., ed. 1978. *Interorganizational relations.* Philadelphia, PA: University of Pennsylvania Press.

Executive Office of the President, Office of Management and Budget. 1982, April 2. Memorandum regarding proposed revision to OMB Circular No. A-119, Washington, DC.

Fombrun, C. 1982. Strategies for network research in organizations. *Academy of Management Review,* 7, pp. 281–88.

Fox, J.R. 1981. *Managing business-government relations.* Homewood, IL: Richard D. Irwin.

Gable, R.W. 1953. NAM: Influential lobby or kiss of death?

Journal of Politics, 15, pp. 254–73.

Galambos, L. 1966. *Competition and cooperation: The emergence of a national trade association.* Baltimore, MD: Johns Hopkins University Press, pp. 19–23.

Galambos, L. 1975. *The public image of big business in America 1880–1940.* Baltimore, MD: Johns Hopkins University Press.

Galbraith, J.K. 1967. *The new industrial state.* Boston: Houghton Mifflin.

Garvin, D. 1983. Can industry self-regulation work? *California Management Review,* 25 (4), pp. 37–52.

Gerlach, L., & Palmer, G. 1981. Adaptation through evolving interdependence. In P. Nystrom, & W. Starbuck, eds. *Handbook of organizational design.* London: Oxford University Press.

Gilbert, J. 1972, August 1. History of DSA's code of ethics, *memorandum to J. R. Brouse,* DSA President.

Gray, B. 1989. *Collaborating.* San Francisco, CA: Jossey-Bass.

Gray, B. 1985. Conditions facilitating interorganizational collaboration. *Human Relations,* 38, pp. 911–36.

Grumbley, T.P. 1982. Self-regulation: Private vice and public virtue revisited. In E. Bardach, & R.A. Kagan, eds. *Social regulation: Strategies for reform,* pp. 93–118. San Francisco, CA: ICS Press.

Gupta, A., & Lad, L. 1983. Industry self-regulation: An economic, organizational and political analysis. *Academy of Management Review,* 8, pp. 416–25.

Hamilton, J., & Weiner, E. 1987, June 8. California makes business a partner in day care. *Business Week,* p. 100.

Hardin, R. 1982. *Collective action.* Baltimore, MD: Johns Hopkins University Press.

Hayes, M.T. 1978. The semi-sovereign pressure groups: A critique of current theory and an alternative typology. *Journal of Politics,* 40, pp. 134–61.

Hemenway, D. 1975. *Industrywide voluntary product standards.* Cambridge, MA: Ballinger Publishing Co.

Hemenway, D. 1980, October. *Performance vs. design standards.* U.S. Department of Commerce/Office of Standards Information. Analysis and Development, Office of Engineering Standards, National Engineering Laboratory, National Bureau of Standards, Washington, DC, NBS-GCR-80-287.

Herman, E. 1981. *Corporate control, corporate power: A twentieth century fund study.* Cambridge, MA: Cambridge University Press.

Hill, I., ed. 1976. *The ethical basis of economic freedom.* Chapel Hill, NC: American Viewpoint, Inc.

Hirsch, P. 1975. Organizational effectiveness and institutional environment. *Administrative Science Quarterly*, 20, pp. 327–44.

Hocevar, S. 1985. Slow dancing in the industrial heartland. *New Management*, 2, pp. 55–60.

Holland, P. 1980. The cosmetics industry: Avon, Mary Kay Cosmetics. In W. Glueck, ed. *Strategic management and business policy*. New York: McGraw-Hill.

Howe, J.T., & Badger, L.J. 1982. The antitrust challenge to nonprofit certification organizations: Conflicts of interest and a practical rule of reason approach to certification programs as industry-wide builders of competition and efficiency. *Washington University Law Quarterly*, 60 (2), pp. 357–91.

Hunt, M.S. 1975. Trade associations and self-regulation: Home appliances. In R.E. Caves & M.J. Roberts, eds. *Regulating the product: Quality and variety*. Cambridge, MA. Ballinger Publishing Co., pp. 39–56.

Jacobs, A. 1985, January 18. Voluntary mechanisms in associations, *Association Trends*, p. 5.

Jacobs, J. 1982. *Legal issues in professional credentialing*, Leighton Conklin, Lemor Jacobs and Buckley Research Memorandum, Washington, DC.

Jacoby, N.H. 1973. *Corporate power and social responsibility*. New York: Macmillan.

Jarillo, J. 1988. On strategic networks, *Strategic Management Journal*, 9, pp. 31–41

Johnson, D., Maruyama, G., Johnson, R., Nelson, D., & Skon, L. 1981. The effects of cooperative, competitive, and individualistic goal structures on achievement: A meta-analysis. *Psychological Bulletin*, 89, pp. 47–62.

Kahn, A.E. 1971. *The economics of regulations*, vols. 1 & 2. New York: John Wiley.

Karmel, S. 1982. *Regulation by prosecution: The Securities and Exchange Commission vs. corporate America*. New York: Simon and Schuster.

La Barbera, P. 1983, Winter. The diffusion of trade association advertising self-regulation, *Journal of Marketing*, 47 (1), pp. 58–67.

Lad, L. 1981, August. *Analyzing peak organizations: A look at strategy in the business round table*. Paper presented at the 40th annual meeting of the Academy of Management, Social Issues in Management Division, August, 1981, San Diego, CA.

Lad, L. 1985. Policy-making between business and government: A conceptual synthesis of industry self-regulation and case study analysis of the Direct Selling Association code of conduct. Unpublished doctoral dissertation, Boston University.

Large, A. 1985, January 9. Attempts to regulate gene splicing proceed in surprising harmony between US industry. *The Wall Street Journal*, p. 50.

Leiserson, A. 1942. *Administrative regulation: A study in presentation of interests.* Chicago: University of Chicago Press.

Lenz, R. 1980. Environment, strategy, organization structure and performance. *Strategic Management Journal*, 3, pp. 209–26.

Levering, R., & Offen, N. 1984. Research interview at Direct Selling Association offices, Washington, DC.

Levin, L.S., & Idler, E.L. 1981. *The hidden health care system: Mediating structures and medicine.* Cambridge, MA: Ballinger Publishing Co.

Lewis, D. 1969. *Convention: A philosophical study.* Cambridge, MA: Harvard University Press.

Lilley, W. III, & Miller, J.C. III. 1977. The new "social regulation," *Public Interest*, 47, pp. 49–61.

Lindblom, C.E. 1977. *Politics and markets.* New York: Basic Books.

Litvack, I.A. 1962, Fall. National trade associations: Business-government intermediaries. *Business Quarterly*, (University of Western Ontario) 3, pp. 34–43.

Litwak, E., & Hylton, F.F. 1962, Fall. Interorganizational analysis: A hypothesis on coordinating agencies. *Administrative Science Quarterly, 6 (2), pp. 395–420.*

Lodge, G. 1976. *The new American ideology.* New York: Knopf.

Lowi, T. 1964, July. American business, public policy, case studies, and political theory. *World Politics, 16 (1), pp. 677–715.*

Lowi, T. 1969. *The end of liberalism.* New York: W. W. Norton Co.

Luke, J. 1986 Managing interconnectedness: The need for catalytic leadership. *Futures Research Quarterly*, 2, pp. 73–83.

Mahon, J. 1981. The corporate public affairs office: Structure, process and impact. Doctoral dissertation, Boston University.

Mahon, J.F., & Murray, E.A. 1981. Deregulation and strategic transformation. *Journal of Contemporary Business*, 9 (2), pp. 123-38.

Maitland, I. 1985. The limits of business self-regulation. *California Management Review*, 27, pp. 132–47.

Maitland, I., Bryson, J., & Van de Ven, A. 1985. Sociologists, economists, and opportunism. *Academy of Management Review*, 10, pp. 59–65.

Maitland, I., & Park, D. 1985. A model of corporate PAC strategy.

Academy of Management Best Papers. Boston, August 1985, pp. 336–39.

March, J.G., & Olsen, J.P., eds. 1976. *Ambiguity and choice in organizations.* Bergen, Norway: Universitetsforlaget.

March J.G., & Simon, H.A. 1958. *Organizations.* New York: John Wiley.

Masten, S. 1984. The organization of production: Evidence from the aerospace industry. *Journal of Law and Economics,* 27, pp. 403–17.

McCann, J. 1983. Design guidelines for social problem-solving interventions. *The Journal of Applied Behavioral Science,* 19, pp. 177–89.

McConnell, G. 1966. *Private power and American democracy.* New York: Knopf.

McCraw, T. 1979. *The business round table (A).* Boston: Harvard University Intercollegiate Case Clearinghouse.

McGlauclin, F. 1984, June 17. Personal interview, Washington, DC.

McQuaid, K. 1982. *Big business and presidential power.* New York: William Morrow.

McQuaid, K. 1981, May-June. The round table: Getting results in Washington. *Harvard Business Review,* 59 (3), pp. 114–23.

Michaelson, M., & Dowling, T. 1983, January 21. *Antitrust implications of business and professional codes.* Hogan and Hartson Research Memorandum to American Society of Association Executives, Washington, DC.

Miles, R. 1980. *Macro organizational behavior.* Santa Monica, CA: Goodyear.

Miles, R.E., Snow, C.C., & Pfeffer, J. 1974. Organization-environment: Concepts and issues. *Industrial Relations,* 13, pp. 224–64.

Miller, J.C. III. 1984, October 3. *Maximizing the benefits of self-regulation.* Presented before the White House Conference on Association Self-Regulation, Washington, DC.

Mintzbert, J. 1979. An emerging strategy of direct research. *Administrative Science Quarterly,* 24, pp. 582–89.

Mitchell, J.C., ed. 1969. The concept and use of social networks. *Social networks in urban situations.* Manchester, New York: Manchester University Press.

Mitnick, B.M. 1981. *Agency, incentive relations, and state regulation of strip mining.* Paper presented at the Academy of Management conference, San Diego, CA, August 1981.

Mitnick, B.M. 1980. *The political economy of regulation: Creating, designing, and removing regulatory forms.* New York: Columbia University Press.

Mitnick, B.M. 1976, May. A typology of conceptions of the public interest. *Administration and Society*, 8 (1), pp. 5–28.

Molander, E. 1980. *Responsive capitalism: Case studies in corporate social conduct.* New York: McGraw-Hill.

Morgan, G., & Ramirez, R. 1984. Action learning: A holographic metaphor for guiding social change. *Human Relations*, 37, pp. 1–27.

Murray, E.A. 1974. The implementation of social policies in commercial banks. Doctoral thesis, Harvard Business School.

Murray, E.A. 1982. *Negotiation: An escape from strategic stalemate.* Paper presented at the conference New Perspectives on Negotiation in Organizational Settings, Boston University, November 1980.

Murray, E.A. 1978, May. Strategic choice as a negotiated outcome. *Management Science*, 24 (9), pp. 960–72.

Myrdal, G. 1969. *Objectivity in social research.* New York: Pantheon Books.

Nadel, M.V. 1975. The hidden dimension of public policy: Private governments and the policy making process. *Journal of Politics*, 37 (1), pp. 2–34.

Nader, P., & Maier, P. 1983. *Product standards abuses: The enervation of innovation.* Washington, DC: Ethics Resource Center.

Nadler, D., & Tushman, M. 1977. A general diagnostic model for organizational behavior: Applying a congruence perspective. In J. Hackman, E. Lawler, & L. Porter, eds. *Perspectives on behavior in organizations.* New York: McGraw-Hill.

National Trade and Professional Associations 1979. Washington, DC: Columbia Books.

Neelankavil, J., & Stridsberg, A. 1980. *Advertising self-regulation.* New York: Hastings House.

Negandhi, A.R., ed. 1969. *Interorganizational theory.* Kent, OH: The Kent State University Press.

Novak, M. 1982. Mediating institutions: The communitarian individual in America. *Public Interest*, 68, pp. 3–20.

Offen, N.H. 1976. Commentary on code of ethics of direct selling association. In I. Hill, ed. *The ethical basis of economic freedom*, pp. 263–82. Chapel Hill, NC: American Viewpoint, Inc.

Offen, N.H. Personal interview, June 1984.

Olson, M., 1971. *The logic of collective action: Public goods and the theory of groups.* Cambridge, MA: Harvard University Press.

Ouchi, W. 1980. Markets, bureaucracies, and clans. *Administrative Science Quarterly*, 25, pp. 129–42.

Owen, B.M., & Breautigam, R. 1978. *The regulation game: Strategic use of the administrative process.* Cambridge, MA: Ballinger Publishing Co.

Page, R. 1971. Organizational response to social challenge: Theory and evidence for two industries. Doctoral dissertation, Indiana University.

Parsons, T. 1960. *Structure and process in modern societies.* New York: Free Press.

Pennings, J.M., & Goodman, P.S. 1977. Toward a workable framework. In P.S. Goodman & J.M. Pennings, eds. *New perspectives in organizational effectiveness.* San Francisco: Jossey-Bass.

Perlmutter, H., & Trist, E. 1986. Paradigms for societal transition. *Human Relations,* 39, pp. 1–27.

Perrucci, R., & Pilisuk, M. 1970, December. The interorganizational bases of community power. *American Sociological Review,* 35 (6), pp. 1040–57.

Perry, N. 1988, July 4. The education crisis: What business can do. *Fortune,* pp. 71–81.

Pfeffer, J., & Salancik, G. 1957. *The external control of organizations: A resource dependence perspective.* New York: Harper & Row.

Pollock, D. 1984, June 21. New film rating expected. *The Washington Post,* p. B4. Source: Los Angeles Times.

Porter, M.E. 1980. *Competitive strategy.* New York: Free Press.

Post, J. 1978. *Corporate behavior and social change.* Reston, VA: Reston Publishing.

Post, J. 1976. *Risk and response: Management and social change in the insurance industry.* Lexington, MA: D.C. Heath.

Post, J., ed. 1986. *Research in corporate social performance,* vol. 8. Greenwich, CT: JAI Press.

Post, J., & Andrews, P. 1982. Case research in organization and society studies. In L. Preston, ed. *Research in corporate social performance and policy,* vol. 4. Greenwich, CT: JAI Press.

Post, J., & Baer, E. 1980. Code of marketing for breast milk substitutes. *The Review: International Commission of Jurists,* 25, pp. 52–61.

Post, J., & Baer, E. 1978. Demarketing infant formula: Consumer products in the developing world. *Journal of Contemporary Business,* 7 (4), pp. 17–35.

Post, J., & Lad, L. 1985. Business-government relations in transition: Innovations for managing change. In V. Murray, ed. *Theories of business-government relations.* Toronto: Trans-Canada Press.

Preston, L. 1986. Business and public policy. *Journal of Management,* 12, pp. 261–74.

Professionals critical of guidelines set for day-care standards. 1985, February 13 *The Indianapolis Star,* p. 20. Source: New York Times.

Ranney, A. 1968. The study of policy content: A framework for choice. In A. Ranney, ed. *Political science and public policy.* Chicago: Markham.

Reich, R. 1981, May-June. Regulation by confrontation or negotiation. *Harvard Business Review,* pp. 82–93.

Rogel, W. 1982. Personal interview.

Rogel, W. 1984. Telephone interview.

Ross, A. 1973. The economic theory of agency: The principal's problem. *American Economic Review,* 63 (2), pp. 134–39.

Rothschild-Whitt, J. 1979. The collectivist organization: An alternative to rational bureaucratic models. *American Sociological Review,* 44, pp. 509–27.

Ruttenberg, R. 1982. Regulation is a boon for business. *Business & Society Review,* 42, pp. 53–57.

Salisbury, R., & Heinz, J. 1968. The analysis of public policy: A search for theory and roles. In A. Ranney, ed. *Political science and public policy.* Chicago: Markham.

Sanyal, R., & Naves, J. 1990. *Complying with voluntary codes of conduct: Corporate strategies for the Valdez Principles.* Paper presented at the Academy of Management Conference, August 1990, San Francisco, CA.

Schattschneider, E.E. 1960. *The semisovereign people.* New York: Holt, Rinehart & Winston.

Schendel, D., & Hofer, C. 1979. *Strategic management: A new view of business policy and planning.* Boston: Little, Brown.

Schoettle, E. 1968. State of the art in policy studies. In R. Bauer & J. Gergen, eds. *The study of policy formation,* pp. 149–79. New York: Free Press.

Schon, D. 1971. *Beyond the stable state.* New York: Random House.

Schulsberg, M.D. 1980. The political character of business in an organizational regime. In L. Preston, ed. *Research in corporate social performance and policy,* vol. 2. Greenwich, CT: JAI Press.

Scott, W.G., & Hart, D.C. 1979. *Organizational America.* Boston: Houghton Mifflin.

Selznick, P. 1957. *Leadership in administration.* New York: Harper & Row.

Sexton, J., LeClerc, C., & Audet, M. 1985. *The Canadian textile labour management committee.* Ottawa: Labour Canada.

Sherif, M. 1966. *In common predicament: Social psychology of intergroup conflict and cooperation.* Boston: Houghton Mifflin.

Sherif, M., Harvey, O., White, B., Hood, W., & Sherif, C. 1961. *Intergroup conflict and cooperation: The robber's cave experiment.*

Norman, OK: University of Oklahoma.

Siegel, I., & Weinberg, E. 1982. *Labor and management cooperation: The American experience.* Kalamazoo, MI: W.E. Upjohn Institute.

Silk, L., & Silk, M. 1980. *The American establishment.* New York: Aron.

Silverman, P. 1980. *Mutual help groups.* Beverly Hills, CA: Sage Publications.

Simon, H. 1976. *Administrative behavior,* 3rd ed. New York: Free Press.

Sloan, A. 1964. *My years with General Motors.* Garden City, NY: Doubleday & Co., Inc.

Smead, E.E. 1969. *Governmental promotion and regulation of business.* New York: Appleton-Century-Crofts.

Stinchcombe, A.L. 1968. *Constructing social theories.* New York: Harcourt, Brace & World, Inc.

Stone, C.D. 1977, Summer. Controlling corporate misconduct. *Public Interest,* 48, pp. 55–71.

Sturdivant, L. 1981. *Business and society.* Homewood, IL: Richard D. Irwin.

Swankin, D.A. 1979, November. *Rationale statements for voluntary standards—issues, techniques, and consequences.* National Bureau of Standards, Office of Standards Information, Analysis and Development, Office of Engineering Standards, Washington, DC. NBS-GCR-81-347.

System buyers push for standards. 1982, March 29. *Business Week,* pp. 138–42.

Tankersley, W.H. 1984, October 3. Presentation on Council of Better Business Bureau Involvement in Television Advertising Self-Regulation, White House Conference on Association Self-Regulation, Washington, DC.

Thompson, J.D. 1967. *Organizations in action: Social sciences bases of administrative theory.* New York: McGraw-Hill.

Thorelli, H. 1986. Networks: Between markets and hierarchies. *Strategic Management Journal,* 7, pp. 37–51.

Thorelli, H. 1955. *The federal antitrust policy.* New York: Columbia University Press.

Three U.S. cycling officials penalized in blood doping. 1985, January 19. *The Indianapolis Star,* p. 34.

Tjosvold, D. 1984. Cooperation theory and organizations. *Human Relations,* 37, pp. 743–67.

Top court to decide how antitrust laws apply to engineering groups' standards. 1981, June 16. *The Wall Street Journal,* p. 17.

Trist, E. 1983. Referent organizations and the development of interorganizational domains. *Human Relations,* 36, pp. 269–84.

Trist, E. 1980, April. The environment and system-response capability. *Futures,* pp. 113–27.

Trist, E. 1979. New directions for hope. *Human Futures,* 2, pp. 175–85.

Truman, D.B. 1971. *The governmental process—political interests and public opinion.* New York: Knopf.

U.S. Department of Commerce/National Bureau of Standards. 1975. *Directory of United States standardization activities.* Washington, DC: U.S. Government Printing Office.

U.S. Department of Labor. 1983. *Resource guide to labor-management cooperation.* Washington, DC: U.S. Government Printing Office.

Useem, M. 1984. *The inner circle: Large corporations and the rise of business political activity.* London: Oxford University Press.

Vickers, G. 1965. *The art of judgment.* London: Chapman & Hall.

Vogel, D. 1986. The study of social issues management. *California Management Review,* 28, pp. 142–51.

Waddock, S. 1986. Public-private partnership as social product and process. In J. Post, ed. *Research in corporate social performance and policy,* volume 8, Greenwich, CT: JAI Press.

Weidenbaum, L. 1981. *Business, government, and the public,* 2nd ed. Englewood Cliffs, NJ: Prentice-Hall.

Wilcox, C., & Shepherd, W. 1975. *Public policies toward business,* 5th ed. Homewood, IL: Richard D. Irwin.

Williams, T. 1982. *Learning to manage our futures: The participative redesign of societies in turbulent transition.* New York: John Wiley.

Williamson, O. 1975. *Markets and hierarchies: Analysis and antitrust implications.* New York: Free Press.

Wilson, J.Q. 1973. *Political organizations.* New York: Basic Books.

Wilson, J.Q., ed. 1980. *The politics of regulation.* New York: Basic Books.

Wilson, J.Q., & Rachal, P. 1977, Winter. Can the government regulate itself? *The Public Interest,* 46, pp. 3–14.

World Commission on Environment and Development. 1987. *Our common future.* New York: Oxford University Press.

Yin, R. 1984. *Case study research: Design and methods.* Beverly Hills, CA: Sage Publications.

About the Author

Lawrence J. Lad, DBA, is associate professor of management, College of Business, Butler University, Indianapolis, Indiana, where he teaches graduate- and undergraduate-level courses. Dr. Lad also works as a consultant through his firm, Prism Partners, Inc., where he advises industry, business, government, and not-for-profit organizations on strategic management, team building, executive development, and training evaluation.

Previously, he served as associate director of executive education and assistant professor of management, Indiana University Graduate School of Business, Indianapolis.

Lad holds a doctorate and master's degree in business administration from Boston University and a master's degree in public administration from Michigan State University, East Lansing.